I[t re, as Oscar Wilde once claimed, is not read at all, then
e[work is not literature or Ruth Robbins has proved him
w   his wonderfully original and provocative, deeply insightful
c   ount and appreciation of the text of Wilde. More than
n   roductory – though Robbins' study is the single most
i[le inauguration to the Wildean oeuvre I've had the for-
t[– here is a radically challenging, beautifully written, and
i[perceptive reading of Wilde. Robbins' *Oscar Wilde* will, I
h   bt, set the agenda for thinking about Wilde again and,
w   to the point, astutely and intelligently. As Ruth Robbins
d   s on every page with perceptive insight, wit and aplomb,
t[rarely pure and never simple, but, in readings such as
t[as they are necessary, it is the truth – the truth of Wilde
a   h that only the literary and reading can effect – which
a   where. As Henry David Thoreau might have observed
h   chance to read *Oscar Wilde*, read the best books first,
o   have a chance to read them at all. *Oscar Wilde* is one
of

Julian Wolfreys
Professor of Modern Literature and Culture,
ghborough University, author of *Literature, in Theory*

Oscar Wilde

Also available from Continuum in the Writers' Lives Series:

Charles Dickens Donald Hawes
George Eliot Barbara Hardy
Harold Pinter William Baker

Oscar Wilde

RUTH ROBBINS

continuum

Continuum International Publishing Group

The Tower Building	80 Maiden Lane,
11 York Road	Suite 704
London	New York
SE1 7NX	NY 10038

www.continuumbooks.com

British Library Cataloguing-in-Publication Data
A catalogue record for this book is available from the British Library.

ISBN: 978–0-8264–98519 (hardback)
        978–0-8264–98526 (paperback)

Library of Congress Cataloguing-in-Publication Data
A catalogue record of this book is available from the Library of Congress. British Library

Typeset by Pindar NZ, Auckland, New Zealand
Printed and bound in India

Contents

Note on Texts and Abbreviations

When Wilde went to prison in 1895, he was declared bankrupt and his household was broken up. Among the goods that went astray was the entirety of his library including most of the manuscripts of his own work. The aftermath of the trials also meant that his life was deeply unsettled, and in preparing works for publication and republication, we do not know that Wilde actually had appropriate access to the tools he needed. In this context, as various commentators have noted, it is very difficult for us to reconstruct what Wilde's final 'intentions' were in relation to the published versions of his works. Even some editions, which he oversaw himself after his release, may – possibly – not be his intended 'last word'. Until the standard Oxford Authors edition in multiple volumes is finally completed, therefore, readers have to 'make do'. My suggestion, for a good, reasonably priced *Complete Works* is the edition used here – Merlin Holland's 1994 *Complete Works of Oscar Wilde*. There are, however, some difficulties with this edition for the scholarly reader. Despite its title, it is not in fact 'complete' – large swathes of the journalism are missing, and since Wilde often rehearsed his epigrams and worked out his position in the reviews he wrote for a variety of newspapers and journals, that omission is a shame, though no single volume ever really contains all the works and remains 'handy'. More serious are a couple of the editorial decisions that make up this volume, which particularly affect the *Poems* of 1881 and Wilde's most famous work, *The Importance of Being Earnest*. Following the chronology of composition established by Bobby Fong, *The Complete Works*, loses the structure and order of the original volume of *Poems*. I for one believe that structure was important. Readers who are interested in the order in which the poems originally appeared have to turn to appendices for information when using Holland's edition. In relation to *Earnest*,

Holland and his co-editors have returned to the original four-act version of the play as opposed to the one which was actually performed by George Alexander's company in 1895, which was merely three acts long. This choice makes the play's plot more complex (it introduces a sub-plot about Jack's debts and his narrow escape from arrest for them); but is rarely played, and probably isn't 'better' than the version Wilde arrived at with Alexander's help for the original production in February 1895. For all that, the convenience of the single volume for general readers is hard to replace, and for that reason, despite the reservations noted above, it is Holland's *Complete Works* that I use throughout this book.

The following abbreviations have been used throughout for very frequently cited works in the parenthetical references.

CH   Karl Beckson (ed.) (1970), *Oscar Wilde: The Critical Heritage*, New York: Barnes and Noble (and London: Routledge and Kegan Paul).
CL   Merlin Holland and Rupert Hart Davies (eds) (2000), *The Complete Letters of Oscar Wilde*, London: Fourth Estate.
CW   Merlin Holland (ed.) (1994), *The Complete Works of Oscar Wilde*, Glasgow: HarperCollins.

Wilde was very worried about the reading habits of the British child in his period. I tend not to worry at all. Whether they read it or not, this book is dedicated to the nephews and nieces: in chronological order . . . Lizzie, Harry and James Andrews; Harvey Donohoe; Hannah Ruth Robbins (it's rather nice that there are two of us); Joseph Donohoe and Catherine Rose Donohoe, who, even if she has the inclination, won't be able to read it for years.

Introduction

Genres are not to be mixed.
I will not mix genres.
I repeat: genres are not to be mixed. I will not mix them.

(Derrida 1980: 55)

. . . [jeune home] au sexe douteux [(young man) of doubtful sex/
sexuality/gender]

(Diaries of Edmond de Goncourt, quoted in Ellmann 1988: 218)

This is a book about Oscar Wilde and it is also a book about genre, an issue that has also been central to the work of Josephine Guy and Ian Small, whose book *Oscar Wilde's Profession* (2000), offers a very detailed inquiry into the nature of Wilde's literary production in terms of its relationship to markets, publishers and audiences. Their focus is on the material effects of Wilde's generic instability (the economic effects, the choices made about publishing formats, and the effects on Wilde's writing practices, for instance), mine on the more traditional literary–critical question of genre as an aesthetic category, though of course the two elements – genre as defined by the market and genre understood as a literary marker – cannot be and should not be entirely separated. The two quotations above signal something about my preoccupations. The first, from Jacques Derrida's essay 'The Law of Genre', initiates a discussion of the ways in which genre apparently stabilizes the written word, offering the reader an 'horizon of expectation' against which he or she can test or judge the individual work. Derrida, however, resists the simple common-sense idea of genre as a formula to which the writer adheres and for which the reader has reason to be grateful. As he suggests, writing has a

1

tendency to exceed generic limitations. On the one hand, 'as soon as genre announces itself, one must respect a norm, one must not cross a line of demarcation, one must not risk impurity, anomaly, or monstrosity' (Derrida 1980: 55). In the case of Oscar Wilde, this choice of words to signal genre's function of maintaining purity – 'one must not risk impurity, anomaly, monstrosity' – is extremely significant. On the other, genre can also be understood as a false limitation on the text. It calls out of the reader particular responses (excitement, or aesthetic appreciation, for example) which may not be the responses the individual reader actually experiences, not least because, in order to have the horizon of expectation that elicits those responses (whatever the actual effectiveness of the text) the reader must come to the text with preconceptions that the text has not yet earned: it is as if the writer has to say, this genre behaves in this way, I will therefore judge the particular text in relation to my expectations of the genre. The material production of a book will also have quite substantial effects on the choices readers make, about the purchase of a text and about their judgements in relation to it. Thus text and reader are hemmed around by prohibitions and demands belonging to the wider culture, which may or may not have very much to do with the particularity of either the reader or the text or the writer in question.

The question of genre matters enormously in the case of Oscar Wilde. As a writer, he worked within and against the conventions of all the major forms of his period (he was a playwright most famously, but also a novelist, a short-story writer, a critic, a poet and to some extent an auto-biographer if the slightly dubious case of *De Profundis* is admitted into the canon of a genre which is itself generically unstable as autobiography is). In all of these forms or genres, Wilde played with the established conventions, and it is part of his success as a writer that he did so, as I will suggest. Part of my argument is that Wilde's writings render genre unstable and often incongruous. Where he appeared to accept existing literary conventions, as is the case in much of his poetry, the writing is less interesting, though even there the proprieties are undermined: the conventions are both invoked and resisted, the rules broken, and this is in part where Wilde's potency as a writer comes from. The game-playing, however, is not without its risks, as Derrida's comments about mixing genres attest. The critical context in which Wilde operated was one in which it was taken for granted that the writer's works could be read as the index of the writer's moral character. Mixing genres, or breaking the conventions in one arena (literature) was taken as clear evidence of likely rule-breaking in another (life). In Wilde's case, there is a sense in which this is true; as he himself commented in his prison letter, now known as *De Profundis*: 'What the paradox was to me in the sphere of thought, perversity became to me in the sphere of passion' (CW: 1018). This is perfectly phrased, as Wilde might have said, but it is also reasonably accurate as a summation of contemporary nineteenth-century assumptions about him. Moreover, it also speaks of anomaly in the text signalling (for some of his audiences) monstrosity and perversity in his life.

Thus, as Wilde's comment might suggest, the mixing of genres in discussions of Wilde overspills textual limits and enters the biographical. Wilde is a writer for whom the critical tradition has focused to an enormous extent on his life. There are many *Lives* of Oscar Wilde, and to some extent, this book is yet another. To a very great degree the life of Oscar Wilde has been regarded as the source of his writing, an overstepping of alleged critical proprieties which Wilde himself colluded in, for instance in his oft-quoted remark to a correspondent about *The Picture of Dorian Gray*: the novel, he wrote, 'contains much of me . . . Basil Hallward is what I think I am: Lord Henry what the world thinks me: Dorian what I would like to be – in other ages, perhaps' (CL: 585). In his books and plays, lives and art have a tendency to get very mixed up indeed: from early poems like 'Charmides' to *The Picture of Dorian Gray* and 'The Portrait of Mr W. H.' for instance, the lived existences of the protagonists become hopelessly and dangerously entangled with the visual arts, in these cases with tragic effects; more comically, Jack Worthington in *The Importance of Being Earnest* is confused with a three-volume novel, with, as they say, hilarious consequences. Fatally for Wilde, the presumption that the life and the letters were connected was a common critical presumption. That mixing of genres (literary criticism with the rather more stringent and serious conventions of legal argument) loomed large at Wilde's trials on charges of gross indecency in the spring of 1895. His books were brought to bear as evidence of his moral character, with damning results. This brings me to the second of the two quotations with which I began.

The key reason that Wilde's life has exerted such fascination on his critics and readers is that, of course, his life ended with a notoriety

– even infamy – that makes for an extremely good story. It was, in more ways than one, an extremely 'literary life', as Wilde himself observed. The genre to which he believed it belonged was Greek tragedy. 'The gods had given me almost everything,' he wrote in *De Profundis*, but, 'Tired of being on the heights I deliberately went to the depths in the search for new sensations' (CW: 1017, 1018). In his own estimation, it is the life of a tragic hero, brought low by hubris or over-reaching pride. For, in April and May 1895, Wilde was the prosecutor in one libel case that he more or less lost, and the defendant in two criminal trials, the second of which ended with Wilde's imprisonment for two years with hard labour on a charge of gross indecency; while in prison, he was legally separated from his wife, lost custody of his children (whom he never saw again) and was declared bankrupt. On his release, he travelled to France, and lived out most of the rest of his short life there as an impoverished exile, under the gloriously fictional name Sebastian Melmoth (a paired reference to the martyred saint who had become, by the 1890s, a coded icon for same-sex desire and the anti-hero of an early nineteenth-century novel by Wilde's relative, Charles Maturin, *Melmoth the Wanderer*).

The reasons for his trial could be described, in Goncourt's words as his '*sexe douteux*', a phrase that could mean hermaphroditism, homosexuality, effeminacy, or sexual indeterminacy. It would be extremely convenient for my discussion had Goncourt been either more sociologically accurate or wittier, and written that Wilde was of '*genre douteux*', for in French, *genre* does double service, meaning both genre (as applied to literary texts, for instance) and gender (applied, usually, to describe the learned social characteristics attributed to the biological sexes). By an unlucky accident of historical timing, Wilde's sexual ambiguity was a sexual identity that had been made illegal in modern law in 1885 by the passage of the Criminal Law Amendment Act, which criminalized all sexual activity between men. One of the things that every schoolboy 'knows' about Wilde is that he was homosexual, and that, in the context of a profoundly reactionary Victorian London, this 'fact' destroyed him. For some early commentators, his life, then, was a useful morality tale, with a neatly pointed moral: behave badly in the spheres of paradox and passion (or literature and life), and you will be brought low. For subsequent, more liberal, more humane writers, it is a story of martyrdom, of a man destroyed less by his own actions than by the hypocrisies of his historical moment.

And readers approaching this book, 'knowing' these 'facts' about Wilde, are also likely to have expectations about what the book will discuss – many of which will be met, I'm sure, because I do not set out to dispute that Wilde was a man who loved men, or that he was a writer for whom this fact was highly significant.

There is, however, something *douteux* about this knowledge and these facts. In the words of Neil Bartlett, the reader must be wary of making a simple correlation between homosexual author (real-life identity) and homosexual writing:

> I begin to wonder in what sense of the word was this most famous of homosexuals actually a homosexual? He was married. His best and most successful play, *The Importance of Being Earnest* . . . celebrates the triumph of marriage over all adversity, brings down its curtain on a trio of engagements, and was deliberately premiered on St. Valentine's Day. . . . the work of this man may bear no hint, no trace of his 'true nature', may be a triumphant declaration of the ease with which we distort and ignore our own lives . . . Nothing in the texts themselves demands that we read them otherwise.
>
> (Bartlett 1988: 34)

It is a bitter question, though much of the rest of Bartlett's book goes on to explain why Wilde was unable to express his 'true nature', through a series of meditations on the contexts of the Victorian same-sex subcultures, and to some extent he absolves his author of hypocrisy. It is important to have some sense of that context for Wilde's work, and not to re-create him as a man or a writer who enjoyed the relative freedoms from censorship and sexual repression that are common, if not universal, today. But if it is a bitter question from Bartlett, it is also one which has real intellectual bearing: was Wilde a homosexual in the sense that we might describe such a sexual identity? The answers might just be: only just, ambiguously, or even, not quite. For Alan Sinfield, for example, 'Our interpretation [of Wilde as queer] is retroactive . . . Wilde and his writings look queer because our stereotypical notion of male homosexuality derives from Wilde and our ideas about him' (Sinfield 1994: viii). It is part of the 'genre' of writings about Wilde, one might say, to focus on his sexual identity as the defining core of his writing.

However, as Joseph Bristow, Ed Cohen, Jeffrey Weeks, Frank

Mort and others have suggested, homosexual identity was a tenuous construction in the late nineteenth century. The legal prohibitions of the Criminal Law Amendment Act had legislated against a particular version of masculine sexuality. The Act was primarily concerned, as Weeks argues, with regulating predatory male *hetero*sexuality. It had been inspired by the sensational reporting in the *Pall Mall Gazette*, under the banner headline 'The Maiden Tribute of Modern Babylon', of the ease with which the investigative journalist, W. T. Stead had bought a 12-year-old virgin purportedly for sexual purposes. Section 11 of the Act, under which Wilde was convicted, did not use the word 'homosexual' at all: indeed, it could not have done, since the OED records the first usage of the word in English as dating from 1892. Instead it stated that:

> Any male person, who in public or private, commits, or is party to the commission of, or procures the commission by any male person of, any act of gross indecency with another male person, shall be guilty of a misdemeanour, and being convicted thereof, shall be liable at the discretion of the court, to be imprisoned for any term not exceeding two years, with or without hard labour.

As I have argued elsewhere (Robbins 1997), gross indecency is 'a matter for the jury', a matter, that is, for interpretation. It does not name specific acts or tendencies, and its interpretation may easily change through time.

This is not to say that activities and modes of being that contemporary culture continues to associate with homosexuality had no existence in the late nineteenth century. Despite Sinfield's argument that we need to be wary of attributing effeminacy, for example, to that identity because of its putative relationship with Wilde, effeminacy was widely associated with non-standard sexual practices, going way back in time to the Molly-House culture of the seventeenth and eighteenth centuries, where male-to-female transvestism was often a major part of the entertainment. When Wilde was parodied in Punch magazine cartoons, in the early 1880s, or as Bunthorne, the aesthete who in the words of W. S. Gilbert's operetta *Patience* (1881), walked 'down Piccadilly with a poppy or a lily in [his] medieval hand', it was his perceived effeminacy that was being mocked, and even then, effeminacy and homosexuality tended to get rather mixed up. Nonetheless, the 'genre' of homosexual life was in no sense fixed, and young men in uniform (hyper-virile guardsmen for instance) were just as likely to be read as emblems of same-sex desires (though they were treated less comically) as the effeminate male. The point is that the conventions for homosexual genres were up for grabs. In Wilde's case, I am more concerned with his writing than his sex life, but there is a connection between them, which is in no sense a straightforward transliteration of a mode of desire into a text. The processes are mediated, not least because this was a profoundly hostile context (as the legislation quoted above attests) in which to speak unguardedly about desire at all and same-sex desire in particular. Wilde's *sexe* was *douteux* because in ambiguity there was a protective camouflage. It did not work forever, but it worked, in part, for a while.

A Brief Recitation of Some Biographical Facts

What follows is a basic summary of Wilde's biography, which provides some of the contexts for his writing. Readers wanting to know more – and there is a great deal to know – should consult Richard Ellmann's biography. Ellmann (1988) is comprehensive, though there have been many doubts raised about his interpretation of Wilde's life, in particular about his assumption that Wilde was infected with syphilis, contracted from a prostitute at Oxford in the 1870s. Nonetheless, there is no better single volume biography. Here, I simply seek to lay out the chronological bones of Wilde's life, facts of which Wilde himself was often rather dismissive, telling his own life story, even under oath in court, 'not accurately but with wonderful expression'.[1]

Despite what he reported to the prosecuting lawyer, Edward Carson, in 1895 when he claimed to be younger, Wilde was born in Dublin on 16 October 1854. He was the second son of William (later Sir William) Wilde and his wife Jane, members of the prosperous upper-middle class Protestant milieu of mid-century Ireland. Sir William was a doctor with an important practice. His patient list included both the great and the good of Ireland, and the peasantry, whom he often treated for nothing, occasionally taking their folkloric stories in lieu of a fee. His wife, Jane, renamed herself variously

Francesca (in private) and Speranza for publication purposes. She was a poet, writing impassioned nationalist verse. According to Ellmann (1988), Wilde can be seen to have inherited some of his tendencies towards self-dramatization from his mother, a woman who refused the plain name of Jane, and created herself as the spokeswoman of Mother Ireland, choosing an Italian name (Speranza means 'hope' in Italian) in attempt to solidify her claim to have been descended from Dante (a clearly fictional pedigree). Wilde's parents were at the centre of Dublin's intellectual life in the 1850s and 1860s, with Lady Wilde holding regular soirées for the cultural elite, pursuing a cultural revolution that she hoped would run parallel with political emancipation for Ireland.

Wilde's education was the standard education of his class in this period. He was sent to school first at the Portora Royal School in Enniskillen, and he went from there to Trinity College, Dublin, where he achieved a first-class degree in Classics. After this academic triumph, he was awarded a scholarship to Magdalen College, Oxford, travelling to take up his award in 1874. In *De Profundis*, Wilde himself identified being sent to Oxford as one of the two turning points of his life (the other was when he was sent to prison). At Magdalen, Wilde continued his brilliant academic career, though he also often crossed swords with the university's authorities, generally refusing to take their powers and regulations seriously, a pattern one might say that he continued into his career as a writer. For example, in the summer vacation of 1876, he travelled to Greece and Italy in the company of one of his Trinity tutors, and was late back for the start of term. Because he had not sought permission to be away during term time, and because he was clearly unrepentant about his late return, the college fined him the amount of his scholarship for that year. Nonetheless, he attained a double first in *Literae Humanories* (also known as Greats, a course of Greek and Latin literature and philosophy).

The period in which Wilde was at Oxford was a rich intellectual moment, with competing impulses vying for the attention of the students. As Alexandra Warwick has recently shown, during his undergraduate years, he

> was exposed to some of the most influential and controversial thinkers of the nineteenth century – the art historians and theorists, John Ruskin and Walter Pater; the Professor of Greek, Benjamin Jowett;

the Professor of Moral philosophy William Wallace – as well as to the work being done on human history and society in the wake of Charles Darwin's theorization of evolution through natural selection.

(Warwick 2007: 8)

These were profoundly contradictory influences. In Ruskin and Pater, for instance, there is an agreement that artistic endeavour matters. But beyond that, the two men were very far apart. For Ruskin, art was a social good, a means by which society could be 'improved', not simply by the preaching of moral lessons (though that was part of his message) but also by the elevation of the mind of the contemplative subject before the work of art. Pater, by contrast, seems to have been less interested in the social weal. His criticism focuses on the individual's elevated state of being, through the subjective contemplation of art as an end in itself, popularized in the aestheticist slogan 'Art for Art's Sake'. At different points Wilde was drawn to both men – both personally and intellectually. But Pater was clearly the more lasting influence, and much of Wilde's work can be understood as a dialogue with, and development of, Paterian aesthetics. In Warwick's view, Jowett and Wallace also had their part to play in Wilde's thinking. From them he learned the processes and implications of Hegelian dialectic thought. At its simplest, Hegel's philosophy offers a tripartite structure for thought: the individual (or the culture) begins from a position of certainty and affirms a particular view; what follows is a negation or rejection of that view. The third stage is not a balanced synthesis or bringing together of the two opposing positions, but an acceptance that both may have their value. It is a philosophy that permits (even encourages) contradiction, and its influence can be clearly seen in Wilde's work in texts such as 'The Decay of Lying' (Warwick 2007: 17–18) where Wilde announces that consistency is the marker only of dullness.

Wilde left Oxford in 1878, taking within him the Newdigate Prize for poetry for his poem 'Ravenna', which had been inspired by the trip to Italy that had got him into trouble in the first place. After Oxford, he settled in London, living on the relatively modest private means from property rents in Ireland that he had inherited on his father's death in 1876, and he set about making himself known in the capital, partly by self-publicizing gestures (for example, he dramatically cast lilies at the feet of the actress Sarah Bernhardt as she landed from the boat-train in 1879 for an English tour [Ellmann 1988: 112–13]), partly by making himself known to the London society via his mother's soirées (now relocated to London) and by becoming a much sought-after guest at metropolitan dinner parties.

Despite the success of 'Ravenna', however, Wilde's career as a professional writer began only in 1881 with the publication of a volume of *Poems*. The poems have a bearing on his life out of proportion with their achievement. They involved Wilde first of all in an unpleasant episode with the Oxford Union to whom he presented a copy only to have his gift rejected in a flurry of charges of plagiarism – a charge that Wilde would attract for the rest of his life. Just as importantly, however, because they appeared to exemplify Aestheticism (the creed of art for art's sake, which went against the grain of Victorian norms, where traditional criticism focused on the purpose of art being for morality's sake), they brought Wilde to the attention of the opera impresario Richard D'Oyly Carte, who was at that time promoting Gilbert and Sullivan's operetta *Patience; or, Bunthorne's Bride* (1881). The opera was due to open in the United States, but D'Oyly Carte feared that American audiences would not understand its satirical message, since there had been no Aestheticist movement there. Therefore, in order to promote his production, he approached Wilde to undertake a lecture tour of the States, to educate his potential audiences about the meanings of Aestheticism. Wilde agreed to go and to deliver lectures on 'The English Aesthetic Movement', 'The House Beautiful' and 'Aesthetic Dress'. He arrived in New York in January 1882, telling the customs officials that he had nothing to declare but his genius, and giving multiple interviews to American papers, advertising both his lecture tour and his own personality. The journalists commented on his flamboyant dress and his artificial conversational style, some with great hostility, since they disapproved of what they perceived as Wilde's effeminacy. After a slow start, the lecture tour was a roaring success. Wilde made a great deal of money, and on his return, capitalized further on his American experience by touring the United Kingdom with a further lecture tour, this time on his impressions of America.

On his return to England, Wilde also began the courtship of the woman who was to become his wife, Constance Lloyd. Constance was the daughter of a well-to-do Irish lawyer, and their marriage appears to have been a love match for both parties. Certainly, after their marriage in 1884, they appear to have been happy for the first few years. Constance gave birth to two sons, Cyril (born 1885) and Vyvyan (born 1886), children to whom Wilde was a doting and very fond parent, though it is possible that the effects of pregnancy on Constance disturbed Wilde beyond reason. As Ellmann recounts, Wilde apparently told Frank Harris (a friend, and an early though famously unreliable biographer) that Constance's pregnancy marked the end of the easy happiness of his marriage:

> When I married, my wife was a beautiful girl, white and slim as a lily, with dancing eyes and gay rippling laughter . . . In a year or so, the flowerlike grace had all vanished; she became heavy, shapeless, deformed. She dragged herself about the house in uncouth misery with dawn blotched face and hideous body, sick at heart because of our love. It was dreadful. I tried to be kind to her; forced myself to touch and kiss her but . . . oh! I cannot recall it, it is all loathsome.
>
> (Wilde to Harris, quoted in Ellmann 1988: p. 250)

Wilde's disgust at Constance's abjection in child-bearing is shocking to us. It speaks of a social world in which the 'facts of life' could be extraordinarily distorted by the mores of the time, which certainly regarded pregnancy with deep ambivalence. On the one hand, maternity was meant to be celebrated as the apotheosis of a woman's 'career'. On the other, it was also not 'represented', and was often treated as a secret, with women going to enormous lengths to disguise their 'interesting condition'. For Ellmann, that commentary of loathing for his wife's body, along with Wilde's first meeting with Robert Ross, whom he identifies as his first male lover, is the combination of events which led directly to the move towards same-sex desires.

Whatever the emotional turmoil of parenthood for both parents, the Wildes settled down to make a family life in Tite Street in Chelsea. The expenses of his lavishly furnished new home and the need to earn for his children meant that Wilde could no longer rely on his rapidly depleting family wealth, nor on his wife's marriage 'portion', which he had largely spent on the house: he had to begin to earn a living. Throughout the 1880s, following the lecture tour, Wilde pursued a career in journalism, reviewing for the major magazines and eventually, in 1887, becoming the editor of a magazine entitled *The Lady's World*. His first act on taking up the post was to change the magazine's name to *The Woman's World*. As Laurel Brake has observed, this change of title was highly significant. In comparison to the word 'lady', 'woman' was increasingly associated with '"commonness", suffrage and higher education', so that the masthead of the new magazine spoke of a radical form of sexual politics (Brake 1994: 128). Some of the typical content of women's magazines remained: there were still articles about fashion, for instance, but these were much less central under Wilde's leadership. Instead, the magazine became the home for a wider range of cultural and political issues, including dress reform (a movement in the period largely concerned with the dangers of corsetry). In *The Woman's World*, music, fashion and gossip were 'presented as trivial and demeaning to women. Instead, women are constructed as serious readers who want (and need) education and acculturation' (Brake, 1994: 142). This is a striking reversal of gender norms to which Wilde would often return, though as Brake also observes, such a reversal need not be subversive in itself, since elsewhere in Wilde's writings, the world of trivia such as clothes, gossip and celebrity are actually accorded serious attention, and regarded (mischievously perhaps) as 'appropriate' activities for serious minded young men.

During the period of his editorship Wilde continued in his mission to become a well-known man of the moment. He made a point of knowing all the most famous and interesting people, some of whom he commissioned to write for the magazine; he was a friend of Lily Langtry (actress and mistress of the Prince of Wales) and of Sarah Bernhardt, the most famous actress of her day. He cultivated a reputation for being an entertaining dinner guest, dazzling London society with his conversation. As yet, however, he had not actually written anything for which he would become well-known beyond the early notoriety of that slim volume of early 1880s poems, and two plays that had met with mixed fortunes when he had attempted to persuade his actress friends to produce them.

From 1888 onwards he began to remedy that omission in the life of a man of letters, publishing in rapid succession his two volumes of short stories for children (written for his own sons), *The Happy Prince and Other Stories* (1888) and *The House of Pomegranates* (1891) – tales that draw both on the oral traditions of the folktale and the literary traditions of the fairy story (the latter being the more literary and 'proper' version of the former, and a genre that enjoyed some attention in the late nineteenth century). He wrote a number of long critical essays, texts that disturbed the canons of criticism both in form and in content, including 'The Decay of Lying' (1889) and 'The Critic as Artist' (1890), texts that were then revised and printed in volume form *Intentions* in 1891. There were other short stories for an adult audience, tales such as 'Lord Arthur Saville's Crime' and 'The Canterville Ghost' (both published in magazines in 1887), which were also collected as a volume in 1891. And then, in 1890, he published his only novel, *The Picture of Dorian Gray* in *Lippincott's Magazine* (1890), which then appeared in volume form in 1891.

This was the text that had, in some ways, the most profound effect on Wilde's reputation in his own lifetime, since it would feature largely at his trials four years later, in an astounding generic mixture of legal process as literary critique. Collections of aphorisms and epigrams were published in small magazines in this period, and there was a prodigious output of journalism and criticism (often published anonymously as the conventions of the period dictated). He also experimented further with drama, writing a symbolist play in French based on the biblical court of Herod the Great and entitled *Salomé*. The play was banned from the English stage, ostensibly because of its portrayal of biblical characters. Then, between 1892 and 1895, Wilde really found his way on to the West End stage with the series of social comedies for which he is probably still best known: *Lady Windermere's Fan* (1892); *A Woman of No Importance* (1893); *An Ideal Husband* (which opened in January 1895) and *The Importance of Being Earnest* (14 February 1895 was its opening night). These plays were immensely successful and popular, and should have made Wilde secure and rich. This, however, did not happen. He earned prodigious amounts of money, though perhaps less than has sometimes been estimated, as Josephine Guy and Ian Small have demonstrated (Guy and Small, 2000). But he also spent it.

From around 1886, though, Wilde had been leading a double life. On the face of it, he was a happily married man, with two children whom he adored, and a successful career in journalism and literature. At the same time, however, Wilde had also begun to explore the illicit and dangerous pleasures of London's homosexual subculture. I mean no judgement of morality in using those words; the pleasures were illicit because in 1885, as noted above, the Criminal Law Amendment Act had criminalized all forms of sexual activity between men, with a maximum penalty of two years hard labour for convicted offenders. With exquisitely ironic timing, in 1886, Wilde had met an Oxford undergraduate named Robert (Robbie) Ross. Ross, it would appear, seduced Wilde during his wife's pregnancy, which as we have seen, appears to have disgusted him. From then on, it appears that Wilde increasingly sought his sexual pleasures with young men – some from his own class milieu, some from the ranks of the working-class 'renters' (male prostitutes who were often soldiers, but who were just as often clerks), who supplemented their often meagre pay with both casual prostitution and casual blackmail of the men who used them – hence the dangers of such liaisons. These dangers were very well known. The Criminal Law Amendment Act was known in the period as the 'Blackmailer's Charter' because of its criminalization of private affairs as well as of public 'lewdness' and as Elaine Showalter points out, Queer Street, which was originally a term meaning mere financial embarrassment, eventually came to mean the financial embarrassment that might arise because one was being blackmailed for being 'queer' (Showalter 1991). Most dangerous of all was Wilde's relationship with the volatile and immature Lord Alfred Douglas, whom he had first met around 1891, and who used Wilde in part as a pawn in his stormy relationship with his father, the Marquess of Queensberry. Wilde was infatuated with Douglas despite plenty of evidence that the young man was unstable, selfish, extravagant and often unkind to his older lover. These character traits were observed widely, not least by Wilde himself who wrote in *De Profundis* of his pain that Douglas, when Wilde was ill, had written to him that 'When you are not on your pedestal you are not interesting', a sentiment Wilde felt left him 'soiled and shamed' (CW: 994). Despite this extremely negative judgement, Wilde could not – or perhaps simply did not really wish – to free himself from Douglas's influence. There were scandalous public scenes, not least in the Savoy Hotel when Douglas fired a pistol at the ceiling in a fit of drunken and jealous rage. Queensberry became increasingly frustrated and disgusted with his son's behaviour, and in Wilde's own words, made Wilde the 'catspaw' of his displeasure.

To force his son to break with 'that man Wilde', Queensberry brought matters to a head in early 1895. He left an insulting message for Wilde at his club, just as rehearsals for *The Importance of Being Earnest* were beginning. It was intended as provocation and it worked.

The message, left on an open postcard read: 'To Oscar Wilde: posing as a somdomite' (Queensberry apparently could not spell, though Ellmann speculates that the mis-spelling may have been the result of rage). The postcard remained at the club for a few weeks before Wilde picked it up. When he did so, however, he decided to sue the Marquess for criminal libel. He had relatively little choice. By leaving the message on an open postcard, Queensberry had deliberately made his insult public – published a libel, as it were; and since what he alleged was criminal, sodomy being illegal, then the charge was criminal libel. In April 1895, therefore, at what appeared to be the height of his powers, with two successful plays in the West End (*Earnest* and *An Ideal Husband* were both playing to packed houses), Wilde took an enormous gamble and prosecuted an English peer. Queensberry entered a plea of justification, arguing that his claim about Wilde was not libellous because it was both true and in the public's interest to know this fact about him. He brought to the courtroom the evidence he had gathered by using private detectives about Wilde's liaisons with various young men, including the 'renters' or rentboys of impoverished London. He argued that his motivation for his actions was to protect the reputation and morals of his son – a pretty specious argument given his own reputation as one of the 'mad' Queensberrys, whose own sexual life probably did not bear too much scrutiny (he was separated from his wife on the grounds of his unreasonable behaviour). Nonetheless, the evidence from detectives was damning, and Wilde was forced to withdraw the charge of criminal libel in case he actually lost the case, and Queensberry was found in law to be 'justified' in his insult to Wilde.

The withdrawal of the prosecution was obviously a defeat in all but name, however. It led immediately to unpleasant consequences, in the shape of a warrant for Wilde's arrest on a charge of gross indecency under the terms of the Criminal Law Amendment Act. Wilde could have escaped prosecution by running away, catching the boat-train to France, as had been the case with the 'outlawed noblemen' of the Cleveland Street Scandal of 1889. There certainly seems to have been time for him to flee. But instead, he awaited his arrest in the Cadogan Hotel (a scene memorialized in London newspaper images of the time, and in a poem by John Betjeman in the twentieth century), ready to face his accuser in open court. And he nearly got away with it, in that at his first trial in early May 1895, the jury was unable to reach a verdict. The trial was rescheduled for a second prosecution later that month, and at this second trial Wilde was convicted. Sentencing him to two years imprisonment with hard labour, the Judge, Mr Justice Wills, commented, as he sentenced Wilde:

> The crime of which you have been convicted is so bad that one has to put stern restraint upon oneself to prevent oneself from describing . . . the sentiments which must rise to the breast of every man of honour who has heard the details of these two terrible trials. . . . It is the worst case I have ever tried.

> (Hyde 1948: 339)

It was a damning judgement, if a somewhat hysterical and overstated response, and the condemned man was taken away to serve his time.

Prison was a terrifying experience for Wilde. The humiliations of being processed as a common criminal – having his hair forcibly cut, being forced to wear a previously worn prison uniform, being required to bathe in dirty water that had previously been used for other inmates – that he experienced on his arrival at Wandsworth were only the beginning. Under the rules of imprisonment, Wilde was kept in solitary confinement. His sentence of hard labour meant the tedious and pointless work of oakum-picking, which is shredding old rope for recycling, or turning the crank – turning a wheel for no purpose whatever except to keep the prisoner occupied. There was a single half-hour of exercise per day, in a yard with other prisoners with whom he was forbidden to speak. The food was abysmal (Wilde, in common with most other prisoners, as he noted in one of two letters he wrote to the press after his release, suffered excruciating bouts of diarrhoea) and the sanitary arrangements were in fact profoundly unsanitary, consisting of a bucket in the corner of his cell. The hours of the day were regulated with early rising and early to bed being the order of the day. Contact with the outside world was limited to a single visit every three months and a single letter in and out of the prison at the same quarterly intervals. The physical and emotional privations were almost more than Wilde could bear.

If things were bad on the inside, they were equally awful on the outside. The costs of the first (libel) trial had bankrupted Wilde, and Queensberry took malicious pleasure in taking his rights: the order for the costs of the prosecution was executed in his name. The Tite Street house was effectively ransacked by bailiffs and an unruly crowd who made off with his belongings following an auction, which was, in fact, remarkably close to looting. His books and personal possessions were sold for a song, and his lovely house destroyed in the process. Not unnaturally, the conviction also ended his marriage. Constance never divorced Wilde, but she changed her name to Holland, took court action for the children to come under her guardianship, and took them to live abroad. After the trial, he saw her only once, when she came to the prison to announce his mother's death. And he never saw his sons again. On his release, Constance made some arrangements for Wilde to receive a small allowance from what remained of her marriage portion, a remarkably forgiving gesture in the circumstances. But she refused to meet him and refused him access to his sons.

A short way into his sentence, Wilde was transferred from Wandsworth to Reading Gaol. Further humiliation awaited him on the train journey between the prisons, when a jeering crowd jostled him at the station as he went on his way. At Reading, however, he benefited from a slightly more liberal prison regime in that the Governor of Reading, Major Nelson, believed that a man like Wilde needed intellectual stimulation and the opportunity to write if he were to be rehabilitated following his prison experience. Nelson ensured that Wilde had access to more than the regulation number of books, and permitted him to write under strict supervision, but with a degree of freedom that he could not have enjoyed elsewhere in the prison system. The result of that freedom was Wilde's prison letter, *De Profundis*, couched in the form of a letter to Douglas, but also, as Guy and Small (2000) establish, the draft for other kinds of writing that Wilde hoped to undertake in his post-prison life. Upon his release in May 1897, Wilde made his way to France, and he never returned to England. In France, he lived a peripatetic life, always in debt and always cadging money and favours from his few remaining friends and associates. Most English people abroad shunned him. He tried to write, but there was only one further serious published output from him: his prison poem *The Ballad of Reading Gaol*, published anonymously under his prison number C.3.3. in 1898. He died in a Paris hotel on 30 November 1900, joking we are told, that he was dying as he had lived – beyond his means; and that either he or the wallpaper had to go. It was a sad and premature death, and along-side the notoriety Wilde attracted for the activities by which he was criminalized, the prematurity of his death has had its effect on his subsequent reputation. As Guy and Small point out, Wilde did not know 'that death was imminent' and he had no plans to die, being still a relatively young man (Guy and Small 2000: 212). His death, however does have the effect of suggesting a certain narrative symmetry to critics and biographers: the meteoric rise prior to his arrest and imprisonment followed by a sudden and catastrophic decline, a narrative shape that accords to some extent with the moralistic perspective of the nineteenth-century critic for whom the preference is for a tale in which, in Miss Prism's words, 'the good ended happily and the bad ended unhappily' because that is what fictional genres in the nineteenth century were supposed to offer (CW: 376), and on which many critics have subsequently leapt as a neat interpretation.

To paraphrase Jacques Derrida, like the law, a life (or, more strictly, a biography) 'demands a *récit*' – demands, that is, a narrative or account that renders the events, contingent and random as they may be, as a coherent whole (Derrida in Attridge 1992: 234). Such an account is supposed to offer an explanation for the events. This is the key reason, a generic reason, for the will to explain Wilde's inconsistencies away. However, even a life as textualized as Wilde's has been is not merely a text, and one cannot expect anyone to live up (or indeed down) to the expectations generated by genre. Such meanings are an imposition. To be fair to the role of the critic, though, it is part of the job to interpret. Given that part of what I want to say about Wilde in this book focuses on genre as an unstable construction, which the author exploited for a variety of effects, the organization of its chapters is also an imposition of order on an oeuvre that is rather more random than the chapter headings might imply. The decision to treat Wilde's works as if they 'belong' in particular genres is directed by two complementary needs. The first is the argumentative one. I want to be able to establish what contemporary audiences might have expected in order to show how Wilde does something different. The second is a pragmatic reason: readers of books in this genre, the literary-critical single-author study, need to be able to navigate the book's content. There were other kinds of organization I might have chosen, the most obvious of which is the chronological. I decided against that purely temporal ordering because it has interpretative implications that I am not at ease with. In particular, it is often meant to imply a narrative of progress (or possibly one of decline). Wilde's work does not fit either model quite so easily and chronology is rarely pure or simple. It is patterns in theme, form, genre and reaction that I seek to trace, and in that context, chronology is a red herring.

That said, it is also very clear that there is a certain arbitrariness about where some texts are located. The critical dialogues 'The Decay of Lying' and 'The Critic as Artist' are prose, but they are not entirely non-fiction, for instance; and one could certainly make a very good case for placing 'The Portrait of Mr W. H.' with the other elements of critical prose, given that it is at least as much critical essay as story. Additionally, there is some adherence to the order of publication if not of composition in this book. In Chapter 1, for instance, I consider Wilde's *Poems*, a volume that comes very early in his career, but I also look at one extended longer poem from later in his career, at least in publication terms, in the monstrous shape of *The Sphinx* (1894). In Chapters 2 and 3 I consider his Prose 'Non-fiction' and short fiction prose, respectively, working through his longer prose fiction in Chapter 4 and his plays in Chapter 5, a structure that has some sense of progression through time, particularly as we end up with Wilde's Prison Writings in Chapter 6. However, there are chronological as well as generic anomalies here. If Wilde began his career as poet, he also ended his career as poet, at least as far as the works he oversaw to publication are concerned. Between times he had been journalist, novelist and playwright, and after his prison experiences he had at least the ambition to become some of those things again, and he might have done so had death not intervened. His self-definition as a writer fluctuated, and any structure that attempts to discuss those fluctuations is bound to be a little unwieldy.

Alongside genre, the other founding argument of this book is about the relationship between life and art, both in Wilde's work, and in contemporary responses to it. This is often a thematic concern as I noted earlier; but it is also, in Wilde's case, a philosophical position and a direct inheritance of the Victorian cultural climate out of which Wilde emerged. If genre is about limitations and the maintenance of boundaries so that readers can be assured of what to expect and of how to read and interpret, the multiple relationships between life and art, and particularly the permeability of the frames that are supposed to contain each of them in their own spheres, develop arguments about boundaries in slightly different directions. As noted above, Wilde drew a great deal of inspiration from the generation of thinkers and writers who preceded him. The debates they had about the function of art and of criticism were centrally focused on the relationship between life (whether social, as in the case of Ruskin, or individual/subjective as in the case of Pater) and artistic production. One of his most consistent themes is about the oscillation between the aesthetic object and the individual's response to it. In a context where critical thought focused on the life of the writer or artist to 'explain' the force of the work, Wilde took interesting risks with some of his aesthetic choices. The risks backfired as the events of April and May 1895 suggest, since there is no doubt that Wilde's writings were part of the evidence adduced against him at his trials. Crossing that particular boundary, between aesthetics and biology, was fraught, but also fatally seductive to Wilde, and it is a tendency in his work from his earliest to his latest works, as we shall see.

Chapter One
Poems

Style, Not Sincerity

In a collection of aphorisms entitled 'Phrases and Philosophies for the Use of the Very Young', first published in *The Chameleon* in 1894, an undergraduate magazine at Oxford, Wilde wrote: 'In all unimportant matters, style, not sincerity, is the essential. In all important matters, style, not sincerity, is the essential' (CW: 1244). Style was certainly the focus of his public persona, for his performance of the 'role' of Oscar Wilde as it were. Both his appearance, as the photographs taken by Napoleon Sarony in New York in 1881 attest, with their deliberate poses and elaborate (for the time) costume, and his speech (the perfect 'rehearsed' sentences recalled by W. B. Yeats, for instance (Yeats 1966: 87)) suggested that the Wilde one met was an exercise in style rather than substance.

For the Victorians, his remark about style over sincerity was not only witty, but also faintly shocking. In refusing sincerity as a benchmark for either his conduct or his writing, Wilde disturbed a number of key late-nineteenth-century conventions and beliefs. One of these conventions was the role of the poet, a role derived from Wordsworth and his strictures on sincerity, dating back at least as far as his Preface to *Lyrical Ballads* in 1800, where he had argued that: 'Poems to which any value can be attached were never produced . . . but by a man who being possessed of more than usual organic sensibility, had also thought long and deeply' (Wordsworth, ed. Brett 1991: 226). For the post-romantic Victorians, the view that one must think long and deeply and express only what one had thought so long and deeply about, had come to define the poetic enterprise to an extraordinary degree, at least in terms of lyric poetry. Another area in which Wilde disturbed his contemporaries was in the realm of the ideology of gender, particularly as it pertained to the meanings of masculinity in the late nineteenth century. As a number of critics have recently noted, what masculinity meant to Wilde's contemporaries was always a matter of some dispute. The public face of masculinity, particularly in its more privileged versions (for instance, the role of the gentleman) depended, according to Ed Cohen, on the middle-class values of hard work, familial and social responsibility, on political and/or social power, on individuality asserted within and not against communal values, and on male sex (Cohen 1993: 18–32). Masculinity was, in other words, a paradox, requiring both assertion of self and conformity to norms of the wider society. Both the role of the poet and the role of the gentleman were intensely bound up with values such as moral seriousness, sincerity, authenticity, restraint and maturity. If the aphorism in 1894 is a relatively late interjection in Wilde's writings, it also speaks to the poems he published 13 years before. The *Poems* of 1881 emphasize the *performance* of both manhood and the role of the poet, not their sincere expression. The critics repeatedly noted that what they were reading was a series of poses, and for this they condemned both the work and the author.

Poems: Lyrical

The *Poems* Wilde published in 1881 with David Bogue were published at his own expense – which suggests a vanity project in part, to begin the process of his self-advertisement and to launch him into the public consciousness. This they succeeded in doing, though perhaps not for the reasons Wilde had hoped for. They were not his first foray into print, since several of the poems in the volume had previously appeared in a variety of magazines (Ellmann 1988: 131), and he had also won the Newdigate Prize for poetry (an Oxford University honour) in 1878 for his poem 'Ravenna'. This particular poem is very much aware of its own status as a commodity, written for the express purpose of winning the prize rather than as authentic self-expression. Because it was the candidate for an academic prize, the poem's insincerity perhaps did not matter as much as the requirement to demonstrate knowledge and learning, and the mastery of metre did. It is a compendium of the city's literary history, spiced with references to the English poetic tradition, and with multiple allusions to the English Romantics, which are virtually plagiaristic, including allusions and near quotation from Wordsworth's 'Daffodils', Browning's 'Home Thoughts from Abroad' and 'Love Among the Ruins', Tennyson's 'Mariana', Shelley's 'Ozymandias' and 'Ode to the West Wind', as well as wholesale borrowings from the tone and imagery of Keats. It is a declamatory poem, written as a series of dramatic poses that apostrophize the city as the repository of literary wisdom and as an archaic (but attractively decadent) vision of an aristocratic past. This past is contrasted favourably with the (limited) new democracy upon which the new Italian state had recently been founded in 1861. Its 'insincerity' is demonstrable: as Ellmann notes, the poet describes arriving in Ravenna on horseback, but 'a train was actually the mode of transport' (Ellmann 1988: 74).

One might expect that an ambitious poet would have been only too anxious to leave behind the 'bad faith' of a poem, which he himself admitted did not express his real views, writing to his friend David Hunter Blair (who was Catholic) that he had compromised his own pro-Catholic position because he 'would never have won the Newdigate if [he] had taken the Pope's side' (Ellmann 1988: 88). But the borrowings, the posing and the intellectual inconsistencies of 'Ravenna' continue into the volume of *Poems*. As the reviewer for *The Saturday Review* for 23 July 1881 noted:

> The great fault of all such writing as this is the want of literary sincerity it displays . . . Worse than [the] profuse and careless imagery is the sensual ignoble tone which deforms a large proportion of the poems, and for which the plea of youth is scarcely an excuse . . . The book is not without traces of cleverness, but is marred everywhere by imitation, insincerity and bad taste.
>
> (CH: 37)

This single brief passage is damning enough about the poems, but the overt critique of the poems is also clearly a critique of the poet, and each of the key markers of proper masculinity noted above is shown in turn to be lacking from the author's personal make-up. These are accusations that were repeatedly levelled at Wilde for the rest of his life. He is accused of imitation (or plagiarism); of insincerity (or posing/imposture); of bad taste (or obscenity); and of immaturity. He is not in control of his material, which is marred by a 'profuse and careless imagery' and is thus a symptom of an unmanly lack of appropriate restraint. *Poems* certainly provoked the official critics, who repeated the word 'insincere' in their reviews. They also embroiled Wilde in a minor scandal, when his presentation copy to the Oxford Union was rejected following a speech by Oliver Elton in which the poet was accused of plagiarism, an accusation that demonstrates the extent to which the values of authenticity and sincerity, aligned with the Romantic value of originality, were central tenets of the critical lexicon when it came to poetry. Elton's speech, reported by Ellmann, accused the poems of 'thin-ness' (or of style over sincerity) and of immorality, but his strongest condemnation was for Wilde's borrowings from other writers:

> [the problem is] that [the poems] are not by their putative father at all, but by a number of better-known and more deservedly reputed authors. They are in fact by William Shakespeare, by Philip Sydney, by John Donne, by Lord Byron, by William Morris, by Algernon Swinburne, and by sixty more . . . The Union Library already contains better and fuller editions of these poets: the volume which we are offered is theirs, not Mr Wilde's: and I move that it be not accepted.
> (quoted in Ellmann 1988: 140)

Wilde, pained by the accusations, responded in hurt tones, protesting against the tenor of the accusations and the ill manners of rejecting his gift, but the volume remained barred from the shelves of the union library all the same.

Part of the problem for the contemporary reader was that the volume does not reflect a coherent set of values expressed by a consistent poetic persona. From the epigraph poem onwards, Wilde's poetic persona rejects what Jonathan Dollimore calls the 'depth model' of personality, that is a model of personality that values sincerity, authenticity, moral seriousness and restraint (and which represents the core values of nineteenth-century masculinity), which he opposes to the surface model, which alternatively values facetiousness and lying, artifice persona, and insincerity (Dollimore 1991: 14–16). In the epigraph poem, 'Hélas!' (French for 'alas!', but also a pun on the designation, Hellas, meaning ancient Greece, with its connotations of both culture and pederasty), the poetic voice describes itself as a palimpsest: 'Methinks my life is a twice-written scroll' (CW: 864). This personality drifts with the wind and has renounced 'austere control' as a mode of being. The poem refuses to decide whether this 'drifting' existence is either a tragedy or joy; it might lead to damnation, but it also has the sweetness of the 'honey of romance'. Thus the tone is set for the volume. The poet refuses to make choices between irreconcilable opposites, a position that the charitable reader might see as exemplifying the Hegelian position of non-synthesis discussed above in the Introduction, but which the majority Victorian audience, on the review evidence at least, saw as the abdication of the poet's responsibility to instruct as well entertain his audience.

The philosophical inconsistency is signalled in the organization of the *Poems*. The volume is divided via different sub-headings. Short lyrics are placed together under section titles such as 'Eleutheria', 'Rosa Mystica', 'Wind Flowers', 'Flowers of Gold' 'Impressions de Théâtre' and 'The Fourth Movement'. Interspersed between these sections of short poems are much longer declamatory and/or narrative poems, some of which have epic ambitions. The section headings for the short poems refer often very obliquely to the content of the poems they contain. Thus, *Eleutheria*, meaning 'a Miltonic swell of diction' (Oxford English Dictionary), contains poems that are political in thrust, dealing largely with republican and Protestant ideas, and referring very clearly to the Miltonic tradition by way of Wordsworth's re-reading of Milton. The 'Rosa Mystica' section, by way of contrast, evokes various Roman Catholic themes, describes visits to Italy, and refers to Dante's view of ideal women on the model of the Virgin Mary, and on the chaste conventions of courtly love. The allegiances represented by other sections are more difficult to pin down. And within the Miltonic 'Eleutheria' section, there is a shift in point of view. Most of the poems there are republican in tone, paying tribute to Milton's poetics and politics, and some take Oliver Cromwell as a hero. They celebrate democracy and violent rebellion against autocracy. Examples include 'To Milton', which is both a tribute to Milton and to Wordsworth, making clear allusion to Wordsworth's sonnet 'London, 1802', 'Milton, thou shouldst be living at this hour', in its opening lines: 'Milton! I think thy spirit has passed away/From these white cliffs and high-embattled towers'. Similarly, Wilde's 'Sonnet: On the Massacre of Christians in Bulgaria' contains a titular allusion to Milton's 'On the Late Bloody Massacre in Piedmont'. Shortly after these two poems, however, the Wildean persona begins to reject this political allegiance in favour of the aesthetic (though not ethical) 'virtues' of tyranny, in the sonnet 'Libertatis Sacra Fames'. The poetic persona may have been 'nurtured in democracy', but he concludes that the 'rule of One' is better than letting 'the clamorous demagogues betray/Our freedoms with the kiss of anarchy'. Monarchy and tyranny at least protect 'Arts, Culture, Reverence, Honour', Wilde writes; and revolt against monarchy is therefore 'no right cause.' The final poem of the section, 'Theoretikos', then speaks of the complete withdrawal from all political, ethical or religious commitment. It praises a retreat into art as an alternative to political engagement or commitment:

> in dreams of Art
> And loftiest culture I would stand apart,
> Neither for God, nor for his enemies.

(CW: 776)

The poems are consistent, that is, only in the sense that they are always locked into a dialectic between opposing philosophical, political, artistic and religious values. They offer no resolution or synthesis to the oppositions they describe.

Similarly, the poems of the 'Rosa Mystica' section are also unsure of where they stand. They tell the story of Wilde's journey to Rome, and his flirtation with Roman Catholicism. In the context of the whole section, the religious uncertainty of the poems is presented as a response to the death of an idealized beloved, which is spoken in the poem 'Requiescat' (may she rest), which opens the section. The origins of this poem are Wilde's response to the very premature death of his younger sister, Isola, who had died in 1867 aged just 9 years. But without that contextual information, one might very easily read the poem as a traditional lament by a lover for his dead mistress and for the beauty that has been destroyed by death. The poem ends with the utter desolation of the poet who feels that his life as a poet is over, for his inspiration and his audience have both gone to the grave:

> Peace, Peace, she cannot hear
> Lyre or sonnet,

All my life's buried there,
Heap earth upon it.

(CW: 749)

The poet has lost the very things that make him a poet – a subject (his love) and an audience, so that there is a sense in which the lament is as much for himself as for the lost loved one.

The lyric genre to which the poem putatively belongs is one which is very much bound up with the illusion of sincerity. Sincerity is illusory not because poets are necessarily insincere, but because a poem is a *made* object (the word poetry derives from the Greek word *poeisis*, meaning craft, skill, making, and Wilde certainly knew this, having graduated with a degree that included Greek). Thus, there is always a gap between the emotion that elicits the poem and the *expression* of that emotion. The resources of poetry – in this case elements such as rhyme, rhythm, diction, image – all require to be worked through, so that a poem like this is in no sense the direct expression of a moment of emotion. For later generations of poets, in particular the modernists such as T.S. Eliot, the resources of poetry explicitly also included the poetic tradition to which the writer would of necessity allude, even if he or she did so only to differentiate their own poetic production from that of previous generations; in his essay 'Tradition and the Individual Talent' he made this relationship with tradition into a requirement for the ambitious poet. Ordinary Victorian readers, just like ordinary modern readers, however, did not operate in quite the same way, using the romantic tradition to privilege a much more direct translation of emotion into poetic form. 'Requiescat' was one of the few poems in the collection that the critics appreciated, and the reason for their approval was that it appears to play by the generic rules of the game, and by the rules of masculinity. It is atypical of Wilde's work as Wilde himself recognized in a letter to W.B. Yeats (CL: 605), in that it is extremely restrained, its powerful emotions contained within a very tight metrical arrangement and very limited image repertoire. It does have a self-dramatizing quality – the figure of the poet prostrated by grief – but that prostration is very quietly expressed. The short lines of the stanzaic form, itself unusual in the work of a poet whose natural tendency was to overspill the metrical limits he imposed on himself, are compressed and regular, suggesting the formulaic representation of a painful emotion being kept under rigid expressive control. It is, by implication, the metrical version of the stereotype of stiff-upper-lipped masculinity in the face of unbearable sorrow. If the poet's voice is appropriately masculine for its period, the poem also refers clearly (and apparently approvingly) to Victorian stereotypes of feminine innocence, in which the whiteness of the beloved's features stand as a direct representation of her inner grace. She is presented as 'nature' not 'culture' ('Lily-like, white as snow'); and she has no self-consciousness that might lead to coquetry or immorality ('She hardly knew/She was a woman, so/Sweetly she grew' [CW: 748–9]). She becomes a figure in culture only through the intervention of the poet's pen; but the poet cannot reflect on this – there is no expansion or analysis in the restrained expression of loss.

So far, the poem is in tune with the rules, both ideological and generic. But there are other elements to this poem that undermine the sense of fair play for the reader. One such element is the fact that 'Requiescat' borrows its stanza form from Thomas Hood's poem 'The Bridge of Sighs' (1844), a narrative ballad, which tells the story of that staple of Victorian morality tales, a fallen woman, who commits suicide by throwing herself from Westminster Bridge into the Thames. As Lynda Nead argues, the poem was enormously popular and widely read, and it came to provide a set of shorthand images for the rest of the century about the nature and tragedy of prostitution and the deaths of guilty women, with its image repertoire being widely borrowed in both the visual and the literary arts (Nead 1988: 168–9). This link was noticed by Wilde's readers. Arthur Ransome commented, for instance, that the poem, 'like most of Wilde's early melodies . . . is sung to a borrowed lyre, but the thing is so sweet that it seems ungracious to remember its indebtedness to Thomas Hood' (Ransome 1913: 27). There is an uncomfortable element to this poem, which is apparently an evocation of absolute innocence and irremediable loss, but which is also expressed in a manner that at least partially implies a loss of innocence. Additionally, its relationship with the rest of the section in which it occurs makes our reading of its tone uncertain. Wilde's poetic personae flirt with the danger of blasphemy in 'Rosa Mystica'. Having established some allegiance to Protestant republicanism in the first section, the volume moves on to an interest in Catholicism, which is closer to sensuous mysticism than to faith, and which takes naughty pleasure in the conflation of Greek myth and Catholic belief. Thus, the tone of a poem that is apparently addressed to the Virgin Mary, 'Ave Maria Gratia Plena' with its explicit reference to the Virgin's prayer at the annunciation ('Hail Mary, full of grace' is the Angel Gabriel's address to the virgin), is very difficult to judge, for the poem is partially about the poetic persona's disappointment with a faith that is chaste and passionless. The Annunciation is contrasted unfavourably with Zeus's erotic encounters with Danae and Semele, virgin maidens whom the Greek god spectacularly ravished, while the Judaic God merely sent an angel with a lily and a dove, and never touched the virgin at all. The chasteness of 'Requiescat', then, looks less ideal in the context of the section than it might when read in isolation.

For Wilde, as Philip K. Cohen has argued, 'love' and 'sin' are virtually synonyms (Cohen 1978: 39), and even God's love has an erotic charge. The images on which Wilde focuses in this 'Catholic' section of his *Poems* are of course drawn from the religious iconography of the Catholic renaissance in Italy. The images come from pictures, and perhaps more particularly from a specific reading of those pictures derived from Walter Pater's *Studies in the History of the Renaissance* (1873). Part of Pater's argument is that the Renaissance was characterized by a combination of the sensuous concentration on the body derived from Greek models with the Mediaeval (disembodied) mysticism of Catholicism. Renaissance art, in other words, combines ideal and real, art and flesh – art and life. In poems such as 'Madonna Mia', Wilde refuses to decide between the perfection of a white marble image of the Virgin Mary and the risqué wish that there is real blood in her marble bosom, so that the ideal statue might come to life. The supposedly stable worlds of religious and artistic perfection, which are supposed to be stable precisely because they are radically separate from the contingencies of lived existence, are consistently destabilized in Wilde's poetic aesthetic through trope of *prosopopeia* (in which inanimate objects take on life). The alleged boundary between art and life is transgressed. One has to read the shorter lyric poems en masse to spot the pattern of preference for art that overspills its frame. In a longer poem such as 'Charmides', however, the transgressive tendency is much more obvious.

Poem, Narrative: Escaping the Frame in 'Charmides'

If Wilde's shorter lyric poems disturbed readers because they disturbed definitions of lyric poets and gentlemen as sincere and consistent figures, then the longer poems of the volume also disturbed the definition of masculinity and the aesthetics of poetry as a mode dependent on restraint. As the anonymous reviewer for *The Athenaeum* for 23 July 1881 put it:

> What . . . impresses most unfavourably the reader is the over-indulgence in metaphor, the affected neologisms and in concerts behind which sense and reason are obscured. Gradually, during recent years, this style has grown upon us, until the poetic literature of the later half of the nineteenth century seems likely to be classed with that which produced . . . the Euphuists.
>
> (CH: 36)

Euphuism refers to a particularly affected style of writing deriving from the late sixteenth century writer, John Lyly and his followers, and in this context, it is clear that this is a hostile designation because euphuism refuses the 'straight-talking' ideal of proper Victorian masculinity. The long poems are long for the sake of it, thought the reviewers. They are profligate with unearned imagery (in the words of one reviewer, 'Mr Wilde brings into his verse the names of innumerous birds and flowers, because he likes the sound of their names, not because he has made any observation of their habits' [CH: 27]); and they are just as inconsistent in their philosophical positions as any of the groups of shorter poems – a fact that was even less forgivable to Wilde's original readers in a single poem than in a group of poems. But it is the story of 'Charmides' that provoked most critical ire, and which, to a very great extent, predicts the thematic considerations that would be central to Wilde's oeuvre for the rest of his writing career.

'Charmides' is the longest of the *Poems* and it enacts all the features that caused most irritation to Wilde's critics, setting some of the critical context in which Wilde continued to be judged for the rest of his career. It is a narrative poem (the only extended narrative poem in the volume), and the story it tells is shocking. Charmides is an ancient

Greek sailor who is overwhelmed by a forbidden perverse passion for a statue of the virgin goddess Athena. He hides in her temple until the dead of night and makes passionate love to her effigy.

> off his brow he tossed the clustering hair,
> And from his limbs he threw the cloak away,
> For whom would not such love make desperate,
> And nigher came, and touched her throat, and with hands violate
>
> Undid the cuirass, and the crocus gown,
> And bared the breasts of polished ivory,
> Till from the waist the peplos falling down
> Left visible the sacred mystery
> Which to no lover will Athena show,
> The grand cool flanks, the crescent thighs, the bossy hills of snow.
>
> Never I ween did lover hold such tryst,
> For all night long he murmured honeyed word,
> And saw her sweet unravished limbs, and kissed
> Her pale and argent body undisturbed,
> And paddled with the polished throat, and pressed
> His hot and beating heart upon her chill and icy breast.

(CW: 800)

Athena, a virgin, is outraged by this sacrilegious act and, when the sailor has re-boarded his ship, she appears to him in the shape of her emblem, the owl, and tempts him to walk on the water (a virtually blasphemous allusion to one of Christ's miracles, of course), before leaving him to drown. The sailor's body is washed ashore by the agency of the sea-gods and mermaids, and is discovered by a Dryad who promptly falls in love with his spectacularly lovely corpse. The Dryad spends the night with the body, believing that Charmides is merely sleeping, and the description of his body fetishizes his male beauty. Her love causes, in turn, another tragedy. The Dryad is dedicated to Artemis, a second virgin goddess. When she discovers her handmaid *in flagrante* with Charmides' body, she kills the unnamed nymph, in a scene filled with displaced sexual violence. The longed-for penetration of heterosexual desire is replaced by the death blow of Artemis's arrow:

where the little flowers of her breast,
Just brake into their milky blossoming,
This murderous paramour, this unbidden guest
Pierced and struck deep in horrid chambering
And ploughed a bloody furrow with its dart,
And dug a long red road, and cleft with wingèd death her heart.

(CW: 810)

The Dryad dies embracing the corpse of her departed beloved. Although the 'lovers' are now dead the story is not over: in other words it goes on beyond its conventional and appropriate end point. Venus, goddess of love, takes pity on the thwarted passions of sailor and Dryad. She petitions Proserpine to ask her husband to admit them to Hades with their passions still intact: that is, they are permitted to enter the afterlife without passing through the waters of the Lethe (which cause forgetfulness), and so they do not forget how to feel. When the petition is granted, Charmides and his nymph are united in a sensual embrace for all eternity.

From this rather bald paraphrase, it is perhaps obvious why early readers were scandalized by this poem; it was the work that provoked most critical commentary in the reviews, almost all of it extremely hostile, with many reviewers using as it as evidence at once of the volume's immorality and of the poet's disgraceful personality. Thomas Wentworth Higginson, for instance, commented that although Wilde was ostensibly talking about Ancient Greece, there was nothing 'Greek about his poems; his nudities do not suggest the antique whiteness of an antique statue, but rather the forcible unveiling of some insulted innocence' (CH: 51). And the anonymous writer in *The Saturday Review* was greatly exercised by

the sensual and ignoble tone which deforms a large proportion of the poems. So much talk of 'grand cool flanks' and 'crescent thighs' is decidedly offensive, and we have no wish to know that the writer ever 'paddled with the polished throat' of his lady love.

(CH: 37)

Even the one relatively positive contemporary critique, in Walter Hamilton's *The Aesthetic Movement in England* (1882), was lukewarm about 'Charmides'.

This poem abounds with both the merits and the faults of Mr. Oscar Wilde's style – it is classical, sad, voluptuous, and full of the most exquisitely musical word painting; but it is cloying for its very sweetness – the elaboration of its detail makes it over-luscious.

(CH: 48)

Most readers were more damning, and for Higginson in particular (his review was entitled 'Unmanly Manhood') 'Charmides' was evidence of a poet whose works and personality were both unmanly. If the poem were to be read aloud in mixed company, he wrote, 'not a woman would remain in the room until the end . . . And [this] poetry is called "manly" poetry. Is it manly to fling before the eyes of women page upon page which no man would read aloud in the presence of women?' (CH: 51). The precise resonance of the word 'unmanly' for the 1880s is difficult to pin down. Higginson, Alan Sinfield has suggested, is likely to have meant, not 'effeminate', but 'ungentlemanly', involving a class valence to the word as well as a gender one (Sinfield 1994: 91). Part of the reason for seeing the poem as 'ungentlemanly' is its relatively open treatment of sexual desires outside the norms of heterosexuality for the period, which the quotations above both show.

Gender and sexuality are terms that modern commentators often try to separate, focusing on gender as the norms of behaviour attached socially to biological sex (what is masculine or feminine about male and female people as evidenced by their behaviours). Sexuality, on the other hand, following the works of Michel Foucault, is used to describe both sexual practices (what people *do*) and how a society values or judges what they do (whether a given practice is regarded as normal or perverse, for instance). But gender and sexuality are implicated in each other as well. For the Victorians, the official cultural line was that masculinity was judged by its active, public status (Higginson's review actually commented the 'test of manhood . . . lies in action' [CH: 51]), whereas femininity was defined more by its passivity and its location in the private sphere. Those gender norms then found their way into descriptions of sexuality where it was the presumption that male sexuality was active and aggressive, and feminine sexuality scarcely existed except as a means to maternity, and that it was certainly passive. As Foucault argues, whatever the actual facts, Victorian official discourses about sexuality focused on heterosexual, reproductive and married sex as their ideals. There were strong taboos against masturbation and homosexuality, which were indexed as wasteful. Sexuality without restraint, which served no reproductive function, was viewed as perverse (Foucault 1984: 103–14).

'Charmides' was shocking in this context because it is full of sex, one way or another. It dwells in some detail on a series of actions that its original audiences would certainly have deemed perverse. The statue of the virgin goddess (passive as such an object must be) is desecrated and deflowered, an offence against religious belief, an act of sexual aggression (rather than manly active passion) since the statue is unable to consent, and a transgression against the boundary between life and art. Similarly, the Dryad's passion for Charmides is active, not passive, thus disrupting the gender and sexual norms that ascribed passivity to femininity. Her act is also unwittingly necrophilic; and the eventual consummation of the lovers beyond death continues that theme, breaking with the norms of Hades as well as those of the living world in which sex was supposed to be limited (in amount and duration), responsible and primarily reproductive. The setting of 'long ago and far away' does not really disguise this polymorphously perverse content.

Moreover, the actions of the poem also spoke to an audience for whom the matrix of relationships between artefact and artist, and artist, artefact and audience, had been a matter of some controversy, particularly when the given artefact is a statue. The three-dimensional representation of the human body in statue form, which becomes a living body (art becoming flesh – or *prosopopeia*), is a repeated trope in literature in general (where inanimate objects are forever taking on a life of their own, at least in some genres, such as the fairy story), and it had had a particular currency in the years immediately before the publication of *Poems*. Statues of naked women, particularly if they favoured 'antique whiteness' in their representation and were hemmed around with discourses of the morality of art, enjoyed a certain vogue in the wake of the appearance of Hiram Powers' sculpture, *Greek Slave Girl* (1844), at the Crystal Palace Great Exhibition of 1851. Pictorial artists turned to the figure of the statue in part because it legitimated the representation of naked female flesh: if it could be presented as 'art' then it was not obscene. Edward Burne-Jones' series of paintings *Pygmalion and the Image* (1878), for instance, is a narrative sequence that tells the story of Pygmalion, the sculptor of Greek mythology who creates his heart's desire in the form of the sculpture of an ideal woman whom he names Galatea. He falls in love with his own creation and by the miraculous intervention of the goddess Venus, the stone becomes living flesh. In contrast with the very 'fleshly' descriptions of Wilde's poem, however, in Burne-Jones' paintings, it is all very innocent, with Galatea's flesh reduced to 'a metaphor of creation' (Marsh 1987: 14). There is no essential difference in the paintings between the marble figure and her flesh-and-blood incarnation. Only colour in hair, eyes and lips indicates that the statue lives – even her pose is the same as when she was merely a stone statue. The perfection of her smooth hairless body is not transformed by its alteration into flesh. It may be that Burne-Jones was reacting to a much more explicit version of the relationship between life and art in contemporary painting, Lawrence Alma-Tadema's *The Sculptor's Model* (1877). Alma-Tadema's picture depicts in graphic detail a much more fleshly version of the pose of a Greek statue. The precise relationship between life and art, flesh and its representation, is very troubled in this painting. On one level it is just a picture of the model's pose; on the other, the pose is so disconcerting when it is robbed of its chaste 'sacred whiteness' (this model really looks like real flesh, in photographic detail) that it is uneasily between what is acceptable in an art work (looking at a nude) and what is forbidden in life (voyeurism). As the Bishop of Carlisle commented on *The Sculptor's Model*, 'the almost photographic representation of a beautiful naked woman strikes my inartistic mind as somewhat, if not very, mischievous' (Ash nd: np). Despite his doubts, though, the Bishop merely thought that this picture was a bit naughty, not actually wicked, probably because a critical distance is maintained by rendering the model in the picture the subject only to of the *gaze* of the sculptor within the picture and the viewer outside its frame. She is chaste as an image because she cannot be touched.

Wilde certainly knew these images (Ellmann 1988: 76, 87). The difference between his conception of the various statue figures in 'Charmides' and the paintings by Burne-Jones and Alma-Tadema is that in the paintings, the boundary between life and art is not actually breached. Galatea and the sculptor's model 'stand for' art because they are untouched by the artist, or because the artist's touch is one of pure veneration, not lust. Both representations of women are also 'unreal' in that they do not disclose either modesty or shame in the face of the dual gaze of artist and public. They betray no self-consciousness that they are naked in public; they do not meet the gaze of the viewer beyond the frame, and this lack of awareness permits them to function as art objects. Art is supposed to be 'pure' precisely because it is radically separate from the motions and emotions of life. In the words of Kenneth Clarke, discussing the distinction between art and pornography, when erotic art incites action, it becomes pornographic or obscene: 'Art exists in the realm of contemplation . . . The moment art becomes an incentive to action, it loses its true character' (Nead 1992: 27).

In contrast, 'Charmides' is a poem focused on the transgressive energy of its protagonists, an energy that enables them to cross the various boundaries that the poem erects and dismantles – between life and art, sacred and profane, and so forth: it is a poem which 'crosses the line', one might say. The statue of the goddess, for instance, despite her existence in the very 'stable', untouchable form of sculpture, is an incentive for Charmides' pre-existing (and never explained) perverse desires. The lines between zones, for Wilde, are permeable. Aesthetic, social and moral laws are made, as it were, to be broken. One of the many lessons that Wilde learnt from Pater's writings was the view that artistic and actual 'failure is to form habits: for, after all, habit is relative to a stereotyped world' (Pater 1980: 189). It is a habit to accept the conventional rules.

The influence of Wilde's reading of Pater's *Renaissance*, in particular the essay on 'Winckelmann' is easily detected in a reading of 'Charmides', a poem of moving statues and effigies. Wilde's poem, though, goes much further than Pater's restrained suggestiveness in his idealized portrait of the artistic and critical temperament of Johann Joachim Winckelmann, the eighteenth-century art historian. Pater's essay compares and contrasts Pagan and Christian attitudes to art. While the Greeks' emphasis on the senses in art is 'shameless and childlike . . . Christianity with its . . . idealism, discrediting the slightest touch of sense, has lighted up for the artistic life, with its inevitable sensuousness, a background of flame.' In Christian Europe, Pater suggests, it has been virtually impossible to bring together artistic, sensuous consciousness with religious (and therefore spiritual) idealism. Winckelmann, however, was free from shame and self-consciousness: 'he fingers those pagan marbles with unsinged hands, with no sense of shame or loss' (Pater 1980: 177). Pater's suggestion is that there is an ideal attitude to approaching the arts in which the pleasure of the senses is treated with the same reverence usually reserved for the spiritual realm. Wilde's poem takes only part of this lesson from Pater's example. Like Winckelmann, whose aesthetic appreciation of Greek art was based on touch (the fingering of the marbles), Charmides reaches out to the art work, but he does so in a spirit of sensuality, not of purity or reverence. Additionally, the poem quite deliberately overlays Christian notion of the guilt and sin attached to the physical body on the foundation of the Greek subject matter, with the narrating figure commenting archly in various asides about the impossibility, and, indeed, undesirability of separating sex and sin:

> Those who have never known a lover's sin
> Let them not read my ditty, it will be
> To their dull ears so musicless and thin
> That they will have no joy of it, but ye
> To whose wan cheeks now creep the lingering smile,
> Ye who have learned who Eros is, – O listen yet awhile.
>
> (CW: 800)

The poetic persona not only conflates love or sex and sinfulness, but he also creates an implied audience of like-minded folk, who share the frisson of pleasure of such a view.

Nor are moral lines the only ones that are crossed. The form of 'Charmides' is one in which a limit is imposed and then deliberately broken. The poem is written in a six-line stanza form in which the final line is always longer than the first five, a heptameter replacing the established pattern of pentameter. Each stanza, that is, resists its own limits. The transgressive tendency in meter is reinforced by the regularity of the rhyme scheme: the stanzas rhyme ABABCC, but the finality of the emphatic couplet is disrupted by the long line length of the final line, and by the constant enjambment, both from line to line and across line breaks. The first sentence of the poem, for instance, which is not untypical, lasts for eight stanzas – a total of 48 lines. And finally, the poem brims with sensuous imagery, drawing on the pleasures of all the senses in a display of synaesthetic excess.

Monstrosity and Perversity:
The Case of The Sphinx *(1894)*

The Sphinx, published in 1894 with illustrations by Charles Ricketts and a dedication to Marcel Schwob, had a long gestation. Its origins probably date from much the same time as the origins of the poems in *Poems*, as the internal evidence shows ('I have scarcely seen some twenty summers', says the poetic persona [CW: 875]), and as Richard Ellmann also suggests, Wilde might have been notoriously inaccurate about his age, but twenty summers implies that he began to compose the poem around 1874 (Ellmann 1988: 34, 87). Its delayed completion and publication have several possible explanations, as Guy and Small (2000) suggest: by the mid 1890s, they argue, Wilde was keen to distance himself from his reputation as a journalist and author of popular fiction; and it may also be that it happened to be something he had to hand when in need of hard cash. It is also possible, however, that the poem, which bears some resemblance in themes and forms to the longer works of *Poems*, still spoke to Wilde's more mature aesthetic concerns. As Guy and Small note, 'visually, *The Sphinx* was a sumptuous book' (2000: 153), and the evidence of a recent facsimile edition certainly supports that view (Wilde 2010). The desire to publish a book for a select or coterie audience rather than for a mass public implies a move upmarket (compared to the volumes of popular fiction Wilde had produced at the beginning of the 1890s) and a sense that the poem itself might be an acquired taste. Having been burned by reactions to several of his previous publications, Wilde did not want the 'common' reader's response to *The Sphinx*. Its significance, in part, although Wilde did not yet know this, is that it was the final poetic publication he produced before his disgrace and imprisonment. In 1894, he offered to a limited public (the general public would have been priced out of the market for this book) a poem that continued the preoccupations of his earlier poetic career. His final published poem, as we shall see in Chapter 6, represents a retreat from those preferences. It is possible that without the experience of prison and disgrace, Wilde might well have continued in the same vein.

The Sphinx narrates the variety of moods and associations evoked by a statuette or paperweight in the shape of a sphinx in the mind of its young student owner. The sphinx's perverse and monstrous shape – between woman and beast – inspires a range of ideas, historical,

geographical, philosophical and sensual, all of which might be understood as 'Orientalist' in Edward Said's use of that term, drawing on
contemporary views of Egypt and the Middle East as the location
for an oxymoronically savage civilization where forbidden desires
might be enacted. Those desires, because they are illicit (for same-sex
liaisons, for liaisons with racial 'others') in the terms of the dominant
European view, are also often fatal. The danger is also part of the
pleasure, however. In the poem, Wilde's poetic persona – just as we
have already seen with 'Charmides' – revels in the production of a
catalogue of perversity, inspired by the art object before him: lists are
part of Wilde's standard writing technique, in poetry and in prose.
The poem effectively consists of a series of lists, which have the
effect of a quasi-masturbatory fantasy in which climax is repeatedly
deferred. The poem's contrasts and oppositions, for instance between
the persona's relative youth (the 20 summers alluded to above) and
the Sphinx's ancient wisdoms ('a thousand weary centuries are thine'
[CW: 875]), suggest that youth is being led astray by an older, more
experienced figure. The speaker believes that his proximity to this
ancient art object will enable him to gain privileged access to the
secrets of the past that she has witnessed. Through her, he will witness
(with rather creepy voyeurism), the doomed love affairs of Venus and
Adonis, Antony and Cleopatra, and Hadrian and Antinuous, as well
as the Holy Family's flight into Egypt. This is a range of relationships
which covers everything from heterosexual adultery to same-sex desire
by way of the most sacred form of familial love. Touching the sphinx,
as Winckelmann 'fingered' the ancient marbles in Pater's works, and
as Charmides 'touched' the statue of Artemis in his poem ('put your
head upon my knee!/And let me stroke your throat' [CW: 875]), will
put him 'in touch' with the wealth of sexual experiences, bizarre and
perverse, which may – the speaker speculates – have been the sphinx's
own experience:

> Who were your lovers? who were they who wrestled for you in the
>   dust?
> Which was the vessel of your lust? What Leman had you, every day?
>
> Did giant lizards come and crouch before you on the reedy banks?
> Did Gryphons with great metal flanks leap on you in your trampled
>   couch?

> Did monstrous hippopotami come sidling towards you in the mist?
> Did gilt-scaled dragons writhe and twist with passion as you passed
>   them by?
>
> (CW: 876)

These speculations also include lovers in more human forms, and lovers among the gods, until the poetic persona decides that the only worthy lover for the sphinx must have been Ammon, the Libyan Jupiter: the poem spends about a quarter of its length in speculation about this love affair before it begins to weary of the scenes its imagination has conjured up. He demands that the sphinx return to Egypt, away from him, to reassemble the limbs of her lost lover, Ammon, from the pieces of statuary that lie scattered in the desert (a clear nod towards Shelley's poem 'Ozymandias'), as if the reconstruction of the god's representation is to be understood as the reconstruction of his presence.

> Go, seek his fragments on the moor and wash them in the evening dew,
> And from their pieces make anew thy mutilated paramour! . . .
>
> Away to Egypt! Have no fear. Only one God has ever died,
> Only one god has let His side be wounded by a soldier's spear.
>
> (CW: 880)

The pleasures of the text's wild imaginings, that is, are reinscribed by the end of the poem first as decadent weariness, an *ennui* brought about by the exhaustion of the imagination, and then as pain and fear. The very quality that first attracts the poet to the sphinx, her durability, leads in the end to disgust:

> False Sphinx! False Sphinx! By reedy Styx old Charon, leaning on
>   his oar,
> Waits for thy coin. Go thou before, and leave me to my crucifix,
>
> Whose pallid burden, sick with pain, watches the world with
>   wearied eyes,
> And weeps for every soul that dies, and weeps for every soul in vain.
>
> (CW: 882)

The sphinx's ironic gaze finally out-stares the poet, who turns instead towards Christianity, though the Christ at the centre of this religious turn is a very ambivalent figure. In contrast to the Sphinx's immutability, Christ is sick with pain, weary, and weeping 'in vain' (suggesting impotence) for those who worship him; belief in the Judaeo-Christian god, this implies, is no more efficacious than belief in the pagan gods of the ancient world. The poet's attraction to Christ, that is, has more to do with aesthetics – the look of a crucified figure – than with religious faith. 'Mr Wilde's crucifix is no less an artistic property than his nenuphars and monoliths,' wrote the anonymous reviewer for the *Pall Mall Budget* for 11 June 1894 (CH: 166). And there is more than religious 'bad faith' at stake here.

The Protestant suspicion for the Catholic veneration of the cross and the figure of Christ crucified is based in part on the fear that the emotion called out by the naked body of suffering man is utterly inappropriate to Christian belief. As Eve Sedgwick has put it, images of Jesus have

> a unique position in modern culture as images of the unclothed or unclothable male body, often in extremis and/or ecstasy, prescriptively meant to be gazed at and adored. The scandal of such a figure within a homophobic economy of the male gaze doesn't seem to abate: efforts to disembody this body . . . only entangle it more compromisingly amongst various figures of the homosexual.
>
> (Sedgwick 1994: 140)

One might have a great many suspicions about the tenor of Wilde's poetry, but one important suspicion is its confusion of religious sentiment with secular sensuality. And because the texts and the man were so often confused in Victorian culture and criticism, there were risks in the stories his poems told.

The *Poems* seem a very long way from the works for which Wilde is most famous. But they inaugurate a number of themes, tropes, perspectives and writing habits to which he would return in different ways for the rest of his writing career. For instance, as Patricia Flanagan-Behrendt suggests, a poem such as 'Charmides' offers an early example of the five rules about heterosexual love to which Wilde would insistently return:

(1) self-centred sexual desire where the love object is unresponsive, inanimate, or dead; (2) sexual activity which prompts violent retribution; (3) the satisfying of personal desire which results inevitably in death; (4) the implication that the attraction that the desired object holds is essentially deadly; (5) the seeming failure of experience to advance self-knowledge.

(Flanagan-Behrendt 1991: 50)

They also showed the way that the critical wind would blow. The emphasis on Wilde's sensuality, his pushing of limits in terms of propriety in subject matter, his 'unmanliness' and his resistance to generic and other norms and rules, as well as his lack of originality, became part of the standard responses to Wilde's works: it was what people expected of him, and in many different genres and forms, he did not let them down.

Chapter Two
Prose: Critical

> Not that I agree with everything I have said in this essay. There is
> much with which I entirely disagree. This essay simply represents an
> artistic standpoint, and in aesthetic criticism, attitude is everything.
> (CW: 1173)

Thus wrote Oscar Wilde in the final paragraph of his essay 'The
Truth of Masks', a revised version of an earlier essay on historical
accuracy in Shakespearean performances, which Wilde edited and
altered for inclusion in the 1891 volume *Intentions*, though he
remained dissatisfied with it and was later to wish he had replaced
it with another essay (CL: 487). I quote it here because it speaks to
some of the key concerns of this chapter with its considerations of
Wilde's major critical works. It states unequivocally – if such a thing
is possible in such a context – that the views of a given piece of work
need not be the sincerely held views of the individual who wrote it.
Consistency, as Wilde was to write in 'The Decay of Lying' is the
mark of 'the dullard and the doctrinaire, the tedious people who
carry out their principles to the bitter end of action' (CW: 1072).
One might have a view, and one might equally disavow that view;
coherence of thought and action are not as significant as pose, or
attitude. The critic, in this formulation, is one who acts a role rather
than propounding an authentic position. Point of view, which is
subjective and impressionistic, is just as important as belief. This
positioning, which might be understood as a 'refusal-of-position', is
important because it undermines one of the key tenets of traditional
critical writing – to put forward a view in which it is at least likely
that the writer has some stake. What this chapter suggests, then, is
that Wilde's critical work inhabits a double (or even two-faced) vision.

It puts ideas forward and refutes them, often in a single sentence, sometimes by the artful placing of contradictory ideas, sometimes by placing those ideas in a broader context, which undermines them. This is a generic issue, since it amounts to saying that the standard generic conventions of essay writing – a certain amount of consistency in argument, a certain focus on a particular position – will not be sustained.

Wilde's non-fictional prose output was enormous, and there is not space to do it justice here, not least because, since much nineteenth-century journalism, including much produced by Wilde, was anonymously published, it has not yet all been collected in a single volume.[1] Throughout the 1880s he worked as a journalist, largely as a reviewer and commentator, as well as being the editor of *The Woman's World*. Where possible he signed his work, but he did not sign everything he wrote. Most of that journalistic output is short and relatively ephemeral, referring back to forgotten fictions and productions of plays; its primary interest to the Wilde scholar is that it also acts as a repository for some of Wilde's later *bons mots* – or his self-plagiarism as Josephine Guy describes it (Guy 1998). It is on a series of more extended essays that his real reputation as a critic rests. These essays, 'The Decay of Lying' (first published in *The Nineteenth Century* in January 1889), 'Pen, Pencil and Poison' (which appeared in *The Fortnightly Review* in the same month), 'The Critic as Artist' whose two parts were published in July and September 1890, also in *The Nineteenth Century* and 'The Soul of Man under Socialism' (February 1891 again in *The Fortnightly*) are the main basis of the evidence for Wilde as a significant (if not an entirely original) voice in nineteenth-century criticism.

Three of the four (excluding 'The Soul of Man') were collected together, along with the less significant essay, 'The Truth of Masks' alluded to above, in a volume entitled *Intentions* (1891), which was published by Osgood McIlvaine. As Lawrence Danson has argued, Wilde's chosen title for the collection was 'suggestive', bringing to mind, among other allusions, Walter Pater's collection of essays *Appreciations* (1890), which Wilde had reviewed on its publication (Danson 1997: 13). The muted allusion to a writer who was, in part, Wilde's critical mentor is very significant, both because many of the views that the essays propound are either pure Pater, or Pater developed, and because in their form, Wilde's essays also demonstrate something quite different in critical terms. In Danson's words, the original volume of *Intentions* is

> a book which contains two dramatic dialogues, the biography of a forger, and an essay about stage realism which concludes with its own retraction: is there a genre for such a book, and if there is, what kind of truth-value or sincerity can it have?
>
> (Danson 1997: 9)

The question about genre is a very good one, and it is one to which this chapter will repeatedly return. Additionally, however, Danson's remark also points to two of the key tenets of nineteenth-century criticism – truth-value and sincerity – which, as we have already begun to see, Wilde habitually flouted. It is to that critical context that I turn for a moment in order to situate the effects of the critical 'essays' or performances.

The Critical Tradition as Context: Ruskin, Arnold and Pater

There were, of course, many other critics in the Victorian period, but this triumvirate are the cornerstones of Wilde's critical positions. He knew Ruskin and Pater personally (he had known them both at Oxford and had retained a friendship with Pater, despite Pater's occasional doubts about Wilde), and Arnold by extended exposure to his works. To some extent, Ruskin and Arnold represent the tradition against which, in turn, Pater and Wilde reacted, but to say that is to underestimate both the extent to which both of them were also innovators, and the extent to which Wilde borrowed from them. In this section I suggest that Wilde's work had a basis in both Ruskinian and Arnoldian views, so that Wilde was clearly part of the historical moment in which he wrote; but he also broke away in significant ways from the tradition that Arnold and Ruskin worked in, following in Pater's wake, and then going at least a step further than Pater too.

John Ruskin (1819–1900) was probably the most influential art critic of the Victorian period. He had a large private income derived from his father's wine business, and he used his money to finance extensive travels in Europe, which were the basis of his theories of art and architecture. His fundamental attitude to art was idealistic. He believed firmly in the social and moral purpose of artistic endeavour, and argued consistently that whatever the intrinsic qualities of any artwork, its greatness was to be defined in terms of its moral direction. He believed firmly in the concept of realism, that is, that the purpose of art is accurately to reflect reality; but he also tempered his idea of realism with idealism, arguing that there must be a discernible moral purpose in such reflections – that it was not permissible merely to show the real, but that the real had to be selected in such a way as to point a particular lesson. For Ruskin, art was didactic as well as accurate, and its 'greatness' was to be defined in terms of a measurement of both its idealism and its accuracy. These ideas can be seen in his definition of 'greatness in art' from Volume I of *Modern Painters*, first published in 1843:

> I want a definition of art wide enough to include all its varieties of aim. I do not say, therefore, that the art is greatest which gives most pleasure, because perhaps there is some art whose end is to teach, not please. I do not say that the art is greatest which teaches us most, because perhaps there is some art whose end is to please, and not to teach. I do not say that the art is greatest which imitates best, because perhaps there is some art whose end is to create and not to imitate. But I say that the art is greatest which conveys to the mind of the spectator . . . the greatest number of the greatest ideas; and I call an idea great in proportion as it is received by a higher faculty of the mind, and as it more fully occupies, and in occupying, exercises and exalts, the faculty by which it is received.
>
> (Ruskin, 1904: 68–9)

Ruskin's ideal is one that insists on the variety of possible responses to any art work. A great work of art is one that combines pleasure, didacticism, the accuracy of reflection (of the real world) and the moral stimulation of the spectator who consumes the art work: what the share of each element is does not matter, but the fact that each element is represented does. It is necessary for his satisfaction that the spectator is exalted by a work that claims to be a work of art. Because he is insistent on the moral frame of the artwork, he concentrates his attention on subject matter rather than on style (or content over form) since it is in content (in narrative painting, for instance, the story the painting tells) that the morality of the lesson can be gauged. And finally, he uses the evidence of the text or painting to define the morality of the artist, which is also, for Ruskin, an essential part of his critique. One cannot, he argues, learn moral lessons from the works of an immoral man. 'There is no moral vice, no moral virtue, which has not its *precise* prototype in the art of painting; so that you may at your will illustrate the moral habit by the art, or the art by the moral habit' (Ruskin in Warner and Hough 1983, 1: 40–1 original italics). For Ruskin, then, there is a very close connection – a transparent relationship almost – between the morality of the painter/writer and the morality of the works he produces, a position of which Wilde disapproved, and which would eventually do him enormous harm, since it is this proposition that made it possible for the prosecution at his trials to turn to his literary works as evidence of his criminality. For Ruskin, artistic values are like social manners, to be compared with good behaviour in polite society. Chaste, regular lives produce chaste regular arts. You can clearly tell what quality of man the artist is merely by looking at what he has produced. And for Ruskin, morality and its opposite are always bound up with sexuality; morality is defined as sexual morality, as he elaborated in *Modern Painters*:

> All great art is delicate art, and all coarse art is bad art. Nay, even to a certain extent, all bold art is bad art, for boldness is not the proper word to apply to the courage and swiftness of a great master, based on knowledge and coupled with fear and love. There is as much difference between the boldness of true and false masters as there is between the courage of a sure woman and the shamelessness of a lost one.
>
> (Ruskin, 1904: 63)

In that allusion to the fallen woman, he makes it clear that his version of morality is one of chastity, and immorality – in art and life – is generally to be understood as sexual in nature.

Ruskin was enormously influential on the art theories of the nineteenth century. His views as they are put here might well stand as the exemplar of Victorian art theory, though even during his own lifetime, Ruskin was not always accepted as a perfect judge of the issue. Following the scandal of his apparently unconsummated marriage, for example (the rumour circulated that he had fainted at the sight of his wife's pubic hair, because he had seen only women as they are ideally represented in artworks, not as they are), he did become something of a joke. And as his life went on, it became clear that his sanity was not as secure as it might have been – he suffered a number of mental breakdowns from the 1870s onwards. Nonetheless, when one thinks of the associations of the word 'Victorian', Ruskin's ideas about art and morality, prudishness and idealism, are probably at the heart of our stereotype of the nineteenth century.

Matthew Arnold's position is in part a development of Ruskin's. Arnold, in his essay 'The Function of Criticism at the Present Time' (1864) and in his book *Culture and Anarchy* (1869), tried to regularise Ruskin's idealistic statements into an objective and scientific account of the theory of criticism. Like Ruskin, he believed firmly in the moral and social imperatives of art, and that it was the function of criticism to discover the morality of the artwork; and like Ruskin, he was also reacting against what he perceived as the mechanistic world of the nineteenth century. Ideally, art would represent the transcendence over the material conditions of urbanization and industrialization. It was important to have an art and a criticism that reproduced the ideal rather than mechanically reflecting the real. But the critic would strive for the real through an objective, quasi-scientific method. Arnold begins with the assumption that artistic practice is more difficult and important than criticism, but he goes on to suggest that without a proper sense of criticism, it is very difficult for the artist to produce his best work: criticism, that is, helps to create the audience for art, a position that Wilde 'borrowed' in 'The Critic as Artist'. And in his central statement from 'The Function of Criticism at the Present Time', he says:

> The grand work of a literary genius is a work of synthesis and exposition, not of analysis and discovery . . . It is the business of the critical power . . . 'in all branches of knowledge, theology, philosophy, history, art, science, to see the object as in itself it really is.' Thus it tends . . . to make an intellectual situation of which the creative power can profitably avail itself.
>
> (Arnold 1972: 94–5)

Like Ruskin, he claims that art combines many roles of synthesis and exposition; but he goes on to say that the function of criticism is 'to see the object as in itself it really is' – that is, the critic is required to speak objectively about what he sees, and in doing so, the critic helps to create the intellectual climate in which artworks may flourish. In other words, criticism is one of the ways in which cultures may be produced: and Arnold, of course, gave us our modern usage of the word, 'culture' meaning the organic relationship between artistic production and the rest of society. In the essay now entitled 'The Critic as Artist', but originally called 'The True Value and Function of Criticism' it is clear that Wilde was responding very directly to Arnold's views, and 'The Decay of Lying', with its critique of realism, is a response to Ruskin.

However, the critic who was most influential on Wilde himself, rather than on Victorian culture in general, was Walter Pater, an Oxford don who, in 1873 had written *Studies in the History of the Renaissance*, which Wilde described as his 'golden book', which he read as an undergraduate, and from which he even learned passages by heart. Pater used the art of the Renaissance as a pretext for putting forward an alternative theory of art from those current from the teachings of Ruskin and Arnold. His book is very definitely a response to their works, and it represents a reaction against a view of art which sees it as primarily moral, socially purposive, didactic and useful. The opening two paragraphs of *Studies* set out Pater's stall, arguing first, that beauty itself is relative, secondly that its appreciation is therefore subjective.

> Beauty, like all other qualities presented to human experience, is relative; and the definition of it becomes unmeaning and useless in proportion to its abstractness. To define beauty, not in the most abstract, but in the most concrete terms possible, to find, not a universal formula for it, but the formula which expresses most adequately this or that special manifestation of it, is the aim of the true student of aesthetics.
>
> 'To see the object as in itself it really is,' has been justly said to be the aim of all true criticism whatever; and in aesthetic criticism, the first step towards seeing one's object as it really is, is to know one's impression as it really is, to discriminate it, to realise it distinctly. . . . What is this song, or picture, this engaging personality presented in life or in a book, to *me*? What effect does it produce on me? . . . How is my nature modified by its presence and under its influence? The answers to these questions are the original facts with which the

> aesthetic critic has to do; and, as in the study of light, or morals, or number, one must realise these primary data for oneself, or not at all.
>
> (Pater 1980: xix–xx)

In the first paragraph, Pater attacks Ruskin's attempts to make a universal formula for the meaning of art in the abstract, suggesting that Ruskin wanted to erect principles that have nothing to do with the primary function of artistic endeavour – the focus on the beautiful. In the second paragraph, he engages with Arnold's view of the objectivity of criticism, quoting and then creatively misreading his famous statement about the 'object as in itself it really is', arguing that all one really knows is one's own response to the artwork. Thus, instead of art being social and moral, it becomes in Pater's works purely subjective, and speaks only of the critic's own personality rather than an agreed position on art in society. Note, too, how Pater suggests – very quietly – that morality is also personal rather than social: the focus is on 'me', not on 'us'. In fact, although this opening to his work suggests an attack on his predecessors, Pater was also clearly influenced by them. It is very clear, for instance, that Arnold's view of the critical faculty also had its subjective element, depending at least as much on the sensitivity and sensibilities of the viewer/reader/critic as it does on pre-erected moral foundations. And the aesthetic principles of Ruskin, which eschewed the 'coldness' uniform classical art in favour of the often strange and weird elements mediaeval and gothic conventions lead very directly to Pater's view in *Studies* that romantic art is defined by the 'addition of strangeness to beauty'.

These relatively gentle statements were provocative to a degree that is difficult for the modern reader to reconstruct. That veiled suggestion that morality might just be a matter of individual choice, understated as it is, shocked a Victorian readership, which took the social and communal values of art and morality for granted. The Conclusion to *The Renaissance* was even more shocking. Pater used his readings of Renaissance art, architecture and literature to conclude that art at its highest level is not social, but personal, and that the aim of art for the spectator/critic is to help him to realize his own personality. In his final statements he establishes that art is not a moral force:

> Not the fruit of experience, but experience itself, is the end. A counted number of pulses only is given to us of a variegated dramatic life. How

may we see in them all that is to be seen in them by the finest senses? How shall we pass most swiftly from point to point, and be present always at the focus where the greatest number of vital forces unite in their purest energy?

To burn always with this hard, gem-like flame, to maintain this ecstasy, is success in life. In a sense it might even be said that our failure is to form habits: for, after all, habit is relative to a stereotyped world, and meantime it is only the roughness of eye that makes any two persons, things, situations, seem alike. While all melts under our feet, we may catch any exquisite passion, or any contribution to knowledge that seems by a lifted horizon to set the spirit free for a moment, or any stirring of the senses, strange dyes, strange colours, curious odours, or the work of the artist's hands, or the face of one's friend. Not to discriminate every moment some passionate attitude in those about us, and in the brilliancy their gifts some tragic dividing of forces on their ways, is, on this short day of frost and sun, to sleep before evening. . . . art comes to you professing frankly to give nothing but the highest quality to your moments as they pass, and simply for those moments' sake.

(Pater 1980: 188–9)

This statement was shocking because of its refusal of the moral narrative line of cause and effect (that one focuses not on the results of experience, but on experience itself, whatever that experience might be) and because of its location of artistic passions in non-artistic spaces (colours, scents, the potentially homoerotic image of 'the face of one's friend'). Pater suppressed the 'Conclusion' in subsequent editions of the text, fearing, he said, that it might mislead certain young male readers, only restoring it to the 1893 reprinting of the text. But it is this vision of an art which is personal, subjective, amoral, without consequence, valued for the sensual pleasure it gives rather than the message it preaches, which provided Wilde with the impetus for his attack on earlier Victorian conceptions of art. In particular, Wilde's essays argue that art is not representational – it has no necessary relationship with reality; art is not moral – it merely gives pleasure to the individual; art is not didactic – it has no message to preach; it takes place for its own sake, and for the sake of the personal pleasure of the reader/spectator/critic.

The Critic as Agent Provocateur:
How Wilde's Criticism Works

The questions of genre and of appropriate responses to behaviour and to the works of those whose behaviours are illicit or criminal, loom large in an essay such as 'Pen, Pencil and Poison', which appeared to its first audiences as if it were a literary essay. Its publication in the socially progressive *Fortnightly Review*, surrounded by other essays on various serious subjects, might well have implied to its first audience in 1889 that it is supposed to be read as one reads a literary essay. Because, as Lawrence Danson points out, that first audience did not know that Wilde would find himself, six years later, in the dock accused of a shockingly sexual crime (Danson, 1997: 86), they would perhaps not have been particularly disturbed by the essay's message that crime and culture can be bedfellows. The evidence of the reviews for *Intentions* implies, indeed, that they were not shocked at all on the whole, and that the game playing of the piece was appreciated for what it was: a *jeu d'esprit* and an experiment in voice. Its playfulness with what might be seen as the ponderous seriousness of some versions of the conventional essay form, therefore, is perhaps only understood retrospectively as having 'an uncomfortable premonitory ring about it' (CW: 910). The slyness of the piece's conversational tone, however, was not particularly innovatory, deriving in part from Arnold, for Arnold made very effective rhetorical use of the generic shift from oratory (essay writing as declamation or exhortation to an implied audience of inferiors who must learn from the great writer) to conversation (essay writing as explanation to an implied audience of equals). The distance between audience and writing persona diminishes in such a context. The traditional essay is, nonetheless, a polite mode that creates its impression through conjuring an implied audience of like-minded readers. Its rhetoric implies that all right-thinking people would naturally agree with the position that is being proposed. It is a gentleman's form, associated more with the gentleman amateur writer than the professional hack, and the gentleman speaks to an audience of other gentlemen. John Stokes has written fascinatingly about what he calls 'The Oral Wilde': that is the Wilde who comes down to us as a fascinating conversationalist, the great talker (Stokes 1996: 1–22). In an essay like 'Pen, Pencil and Poison', the oral Wilde gets written down, we might say.

Wilde describes 'Pen, Pencil and Poison' within the text as a 'brief memoir' – an essay, that is, which remembers a particular figure. (The contemporary sense of 'memoir', meaning personal reminiscence, was not at this point the most usual meaning of the word.) But straightaway, the subject of the memoir distorts the polite world of the traditional essay form. For, as we are told in the first paragraph, Thomas Griffiths Wainewright was not only a

> poet and a painter, an art-critic, an antiquarian, and a writer of prose, an amateur of beautiful things and a dilettante of things delightful, but [was] also a forger of no mean or ordinary capabilities, and as a subtle and secret poisoner, almost without rival in this or any age.
>
> (CW: 1093)

The first part of the sentence evokes the traditional subject matter of the polite memoir essay; the second part is an absolute deflation of that tradition. The two parts of the sentence – as indeed is the case with the two parts of Wainewright himself, art and crime – do not belong together. There is a dramatic inconsistency in the values signalled by the writing. I have argued elsewhere that the description of Wainewright's childhood undermines the romantic myth of childhood as innocent and perfect, and undoes the causal link between childhood happiness and moral propriety, which the Victorians valued in their post-romantic way (Robbins 2003: 123–5). Here, the satire is not aimed entirely at the reader, though obviously it rebounds on the audience's generic expectation and assumptions; but more precisely, it debunks the genre, the very possibility of a polite (if one-sided) written conversation between like-minded folk. We are also asked to accept Wainewright as an artistic and a moral equal to Rubens, Goethe, Milton and Sophocles, a comparison that elevates Wainewright, but also debunks the unquestioned value apportioned to those other great names. The genre in which the text is apparently written asks us to accept forgery and poisoning as equivalent values to art, not as oppositions to it. The very concept of art as a value is threatened in this juxtaposition. The reader is unable to judge the tone. Is this a joke? Or does the writing persona seriously propose that criminality itself might be an art form?

The polite surface of the essay contains some very pointed allusions

and phrases. Discussing Wainewright's career as an art critic, for
instance, Wilde's critical persona remarks:

> As an art-critic he concerned himself primarily with the complex
> impressions produced by a work of art, and certainly the first step
> in aesthetic criticism is to realise one's own impressions. He cared
> nothing for abstract discussions on the nature of the Beautiful, and
> the historical method, which has since yielded such rich fruit, did not
> belong to his day, but he never lost sight of the great truth that Art's
> first appeal is neither to the intellect nor to the emotions, but purely to
> the artistic temperament, this 'taste' as he calls it, being unconsciously
> guided and made perfect by frequent contact with the best work,
> becomes in the end a form of right judgement.
>
> (CW: 1096)

In that passage, there is a gentle nudge at Pater (whose phrase 'the
first step in aesthetic criticism . . .' is directly lifted from *Studies in the
History of the Renaissance*); a poke at Ruskin's abstractions; a dig at the
historical methods for criticism derived from the historical exegesis of
the Bible exemplified by Strauss's *Leben Jesu* (*The Life of Jesus*, translated
into English by George Eliot in 1846); and a clear allusion to Arnold's
view that criticism is about the recognition of the 'best work' ('the best
that has been thought and said', and his metaphor of the 'touchstone'
of 'great works', which enable the reader to measure value). Major
figures are quoted in mischievous juxtaposition that disguises their
logical and philosophical differences in the service of an argument
that states that a convicted poisoner's 'taste' is as good a measure of
artistic value as any other. It may be a joke (or maybe not); but the
essay appears to suggest that morality is indeed personal, not social.

Juxtaposition of unlikely sentence- and paragraph-fellows is the
essay's technique. The surface message of the Wainewright memoir
is that the poisoner was highly skilled with pen and pencil: in other
words he was both a gifted artist and eloquent writer. Wilde's com-
mentaries on Wainewright's writing, however, are barbed. Having
quoted at length one of his subject's descriptions of a painting, he
writes: 'Were this description carefully rewritten, it would be quite
admirable' (CW: 1100). And later he goes on to say of Wainewright's
prose style (under the pseudonym Janus Weathercock, a name he used
for newspaper publication):

He was the pioneer of Asiatic prose, and delighted in pictorial epithets and pompous exaggerations. To have a style so gorgeous that it conceals the subject is one of the highest achievements of an important and admired school of Fleet Street leader-writers . . . He also saw that it was quite easy by continued reiteration, to make the public interested in his own personality, and in his purely journalistic articles this extraordinary young man tells the world what he had for dinner, where he gets his clothes, what wines he likes . . . just as if he were writing weekly notes for some popular newspaper of our own time. This being the least valuable part of his work, is the one that has had the most obvious influence. A publicist, nowadays, is a man who bores the community with the details of the illegalities of his private life.

(CW: 1101)

In a passage like this, Wilde shows that the joke is also at his own expense. The descriptions of Wainewright's overwrought prose style are indirectly borrowed from the critical responses to Wilde's own prose fiction (*The Happy Prince and Other Tales* had been published the previous year, with some hostile commentary on Wilde's prose style). And the remarks about Wainewright's self-publicity are very clearly levelled by Wilde at Wilde himself. Only the remark about the 'illegalities of his private life' is particularly risky, especially read with the retrospective knowledge of what befell Wilde in 1895. Thus, although I agree with Danson's commentary that the original audiences would not necessarily have been reading Wilde's memoir as a particularly risqué or even risky piece of self-positioning, it is at least possible that a coterie audience of his associates would have recognized a commentary that spoke particularly to them. To connect oneself, even if only in terms of prose style and subject matter, with a murderer, is quite a leap.

In discussing Wainewright's artistic production, the effects of comic juxtaposition are re-emphasized. The murders Wainewright committed are reduced in significance by the very tiny amount of space each is accorded and by their subordination to the narrative of the artist. When Wainewright poisoned the father of one of his lady friends, for example, we are told: 'His friend died the next day in his presence, and he left Boulogne at once for a sketching tour through the most picturesque parts of Brittany' (CW: 1103). More space is given to the details of his lodgings in Northern France than to the killing. Again, in the description of his poisoning of his sister-in-law, it is the artist that matters more than the killer:

> A very charming red-chalk drawing of [the murder victim] by her brother-in law is still in existence, and shows how much his style as an artist was influenced by Sir Thomas Lawrence, a painter for whose work he had always entertained a great admiration. De Quincey says that Mrs. Wainewright was not really privy to the murder. Let us hope that she was not. Sin should be solitary, and have no accomplices.
>
> (CW: 1103)

His motive for this particular murder was the victim's 'thick ankles', an aesthetic motive, but one that shows the extent to which the motive does not fit the crime. Just as importantly in that passage, is the sneakily naughty remark about solitary sin – 'solitary vice' was of course the nineteenth-century euphemism for masturbatory practices, a reference to which Wilde has smuggled in to the apparently urbane context of the polite essay form. What we are seeing here is a doubleness on several different levels. A double audience is addressed (a knowing audience, a more innocent one); a double voice is used – a polite voice that says outrageous things; and there is also a double attitude, which will be repeated in other of Wilde's works – parody, (mis)quotation, allusion and other references are made to do the double service of paying a homage to Wilde's critical ancestors and also to measure his distance from them.

The doubleness of 'Pen, Pencil and Poison' and its author's veiled self-referentiality, which breaks the frame of the essay genre, are both written much larger in the two critical dialogues, 'The Decay of Lying' and the two parts of 'The Critic as Artist'. Wilde's 'conversational' style and his desire to hold contradictory positions find their logical form of expression in the dialogues. This motive is inscribed into 'The Critic as Artist' where the two interlocutors actually discuss the generic advantages of the form in which their essay conversation has taken place. The critic, says Gilbert, 'may use dialogue' rather than being limited to 'the subjective form of expression' implied by a single voice. 'By its means he can both reveal and conceal himself . . . By its means he can exhibit the object from each point of view, and show it to us in the round, as a sculptor shows us things' (CW: 1143). And, by its means, comments Ernest playfully, 'he can invent an imaginary antagonist, and convert him when he chooses by some absurdly sophistical argument' (CW: 1143). Danson describes this moment as 'frame breaking' (Danson 1997: 36), a disruption of the generic conventions of the dialogue, where the external audience is required to 'suspend disbelief' in the reality of the conversation taking place on the page/stage. The reference to the art of sculpture is also significant. The three-dimensional figure (a single pose or attitude) that comes to life (and thus multiplies the poses and attitudes it can represent and inhabit), we have already seen in the discussion of 'Charmides', is a trope in which Wilde was very early interested and to which he would return. The art/life dichotomy is writ large in these two conversational dialogues, in which conversation is itself an art form which enriches the real, a view that Wilde had propounded in a review of J. P. Mahaffy's *The Principles of the Art of Conversation* in 1887 (CW: 970–2).

Wilde's policy in 'The Decay of Lying' and 'The Critic as Artist' is to upend his readers' expectations and conventions. His frivolity is, in fact, very serious, for by turning round those expectations, he forces a reappraisal of ideas that have perhaps become merely habitual, having taken Pater at his word, that failure, whether of behaviour or of belief, is to form habits. Wilde uses a terminology that is ethically loaded, in his society, but disrupts the valuation of that ethical loading. As Jonathan Dollimore suggests, in the list below, there were positive and negative values that were taken for granted in the late Victorian period as indices of good character. The 'Y' list was more usually the privileged and preferred set of values. Wilde, however, replaces the negative term with the positive and vice versa:

X	for	Y
surface		depth
lying		truth
change		stasis
difference		essence
persona/role		essential self
abnormal		normal
insincerity		sincerity
style/artifice		authenticity
facetious		serious
narcissism		maturity

(Dollimore 1991: 15)

Dollimore describes the upending of expected values a process of inversion and perversion, using these words positively as part of a larger argument about Wilde's desire to write a cultural space for gay men in a society that saw them as outlaws; but he also goes on to say that such inversions have cultural effects beyond the particularity of homosexuality, because they demonstrate that all such ethically loaded binary oppositions are constructed rather than self-evidently and transparently true. Whatever the sexual politics (and there is a great deal in Dollimore's argument), this 'queering' of the ethical pitch is not only a message for a coterie audience of men who love men.

In 'The Decay of Lying', two young men (Cyril and Vivian – the names, of course, of Wilde's two sons, at this point aged 2 and 3 years old) stay up all night smoking cigarettes and discussing the meaning of art. The dialogue opens with Cyril's invitation to Vivian to come outside, which may or may not be a seductive 'come on':

> My dear Vivian, don't coop yourself up all day in the library. It is a perfectly lovely afternoon. The air is exquisite. There is a mist upon the woods, like the purple bloom upon a plum. Let us go and lie on the grass, and smoke cigarettes, and enjoy Nature.
>
> (CW: 1071)

Vivian's response is that no cultivated person could possibly enjoy nature; nature is uncomfortable, there are always insects, and frankly nature does not have the attractions of either Oxford Street (which stands for the pleasures of the city), nor of art; nature is uncomfortable and inartistic compared to the perfections of an urban drawing room. That is, in a post-romantic era during which, following the strictures of Wordsworth, the privileged term is always 'nature', Wilde has his mouthpiece personality reverse the values of the terms in the binary opposition, preferring the urban to the rural, and the artificial to the natural. And there's a more important reason than even the one he has just suggested; worse still, nature is too big, and it does not allow the personality to be expressed – it has no sense of proportion:

> I prefer houses to open air. In a house we feel all of the proper proportions. Everything is subordinated to us, fashioned for our use and our pleasure. Egotism itself which is so necessary to a proper sense

of human dignity, is entirely the result of indoor life. Out of doors one becomes abstract and impersonal. One's individuality leaves one.
(CW: 1071)

Personality is all important to Wilde. It is his preferred word over other more 'Victorian' descriptions of subjectivity (for instance, character). Personality, deriving from the Latin word *persona* meaning 'mask', is a surface thing, different from character, which is meant to represent the essential self. Personality is something one acts; character is something one is. And this falsified personality fits in with everything which Vivian is going to say about lying and why it is necessary.

'The Decay of Lying' has as its focus a debate about realism in the arts. This was a very topical subject, which had been discussed back and forth in the pages of various journals in the 1880s and which would continue well beyond into the 90s (see, for example, Ledger and Luckhurst 2000: 97–130). But as well as that topical reference, alongside Cyril and Vivian there is a third implied interlocutor: John Ruskin with his focus on the 'real' and on idealized realism, and his insistence on the primacy of nature. The dialogue does not invest the concept of lying with any ethical meaning; lying, by semantic sleight of hand comes simply to stand for art and artifice. 'After all, what is a fine lie?' asks Vivian. 'Simply that which is its own evidence' (CW: 1072). Lying defines art itself, for Wilde, following the French poet and novelist Gautier, would believe that art takes place only for its own sake – it has no function beyond itself. A lie is perfect when it is totally consistent and coherent, like a beautiful object. It ceases to be beautiful, and therefore artistic, when it becomes useful, when it's a lie told for a purpose. Thus politicians' lies don't count in this definition because they have a life beyond themselves.

From there, Vivian goes on to discuss some of the most famous writers of the day, often with caustic wit, and to explain why their continued commitment to Realism makes it virtually impossible to read their works. His argument is that great literature is invented and unnatural (or artificial). The artifice of poetry is a great craft that has to be learned and practised, as opposed to being innate:

> People have a careless way of talking about a 'born liar' just as they talk about a born poet. But in both cases they are wrong. . . . As one knows the poet by his fine music, so one can recognise the liar by his

rich rhythmic utterance, and in neither case will the casual inspiration
of the moment suffice . . . practice must precede perfection.

(CW: 1073)

The artificiality of art is its glory. The adherence to nature, for
instance, is responsible for the worst of Wordsworth's verse; it was
the adherence to poetry (its craft, its labour, its technique) that gave
him his greatest poems (CW: 1078). The anti-romantic position not
only explicitly attacks Wordsworth, but also implicitly pokes fun at
Ruskin's Wordsworthian preferences.

In a move that it is very typical of Wilde, and which will be
repeated in 'The Critic as Artist', the next proposition is that art
does not imitate nature as much as nature imitates art: this is a direct
reversal of almost any commonsensical position, a flourish of illogic-
ality that Vivian then takes great pleasure in defending.

Where, if not from the Impressionists, do we get those wonderful
brown fogs that come creeping down our streets, blurring the gas-
lamps and changing the houses into monstrous shadows? To whom,
if not to them and their master, do we owe the lovely silver mists that
brood over our river, and turn to faint forms of fading grace curved
bridge and swaying barge? The extraordinary change that has taken
place in the climate of London during the last ten years is entirely
due to this particular school of Art. You smile. Consider the matter
from a scientific or a metaphysical point of view, and you will find
that I am right. For what is Nature? Nature is no great mother who
has borne us. She is our creation. It is in our brain that she quickens
to life. *Things are because we see them*, and what we see, and how we
see it, depends on the Arts that have influenced us.

(CW: 1086, my emphasis)

This is couched in terms that seem to be quite frivolous, but Wilde is,
of course, getting Vivian to make a number of serious points: about
the subjective nature of reality (in the emphasized phrase); about the
'habit' of mind that unquestioningly accepts the romantic appreciation of nature; and about the effects of a common culture on the
perception of nature. The examples and the rhetorical flourishes are
summarized at the end of the dialogue with Vivian expounding his
four doctrines about art:

Art never expresses anything but itself. . . . All bad art comes from returning to Life and Nature, and elevating them into ideals. . . . Life imitates Art far more than Art imitates Life . . . Lying, the telling of beautiful untrue things, is the proper aim of art.

(CW: 1091)

But ironically from his original refusal to smoke cigarettes among the glories of nature, Vivian ends his piece precisely by inviting Cyril to do just that:

But of this, I think that I have spoken at sufficient length. And now let us go onto the terrace, where 'droops the milk-white peacock like a ghost', while the evening star 'washes the dusk with silver'. At twilight, nature becomes a wonderfully suggestive effect, and is not without its loveliness, though perhaps its chief use is to illustrate quotations from the poets. Come! We have talked long enough.

(CW: 1092)

The two quotations from the poets are from Tennyson and Blake, and they are included in the invitation to go outside because they illustrate (though they do not prove) Vivian's contention that our view of nature has been formed by the arts that have influenced us.

'The Critic as Artist' continues the debate in other terms and with other conversationalists. In this case, the internal characters are Gilbert and Ernest and the implied interlocutor is Arnold. 'Critic' represents at once a homage to Arnold while also dramatizing the rejection of his views and his personal preoccupations. What the dialogue takes from Arnold is the view that criticism is extremely important if one wishes for the arts to flourish. In his essay 'The Function of Criticism at the Present Time', Arnold had written of the importance of criticism in European culture, and lamented the failure of English literature to make use of the critical spirit. What criticism offers, he wrote is the capacity to:

make an intellectual situation of which the creative power can profitably avail itself. It tends to establish an order of ideas, if not absolutely true, yet true by comparison with that which it displaces; to make the best ideas prevail. Presently these new ideas reach society, the touch of truth is the touch of life, and there is a stir and growth everywhere; out of this stir and growth come the creative epochs of literature.

(Arnold 1972: 134)

The importance that Arnold accords to criticism is what Wilde takes from his writing, though he takes it rather further, perhaps, than Arnold ever intended. But the other element in this quotation is the social usefulness that Arnold accords to criticism: new ideas reach society – which has its effect on literature, but which also has its effects on the social world more generally. That social purpose is what Wilde rejects, with a series of pointed comments, some of which are clearly directly aimed at the recently deceased Arnold, who had only died in April 1888. In particular, there are barbs aimed at the development of state-run formal education in which Arnold had played a significant part, in his role as a government inspector of schools in the 1850s and beyond. (Wilde may have been jealous of this appointment; he had also applied for a similar role after graduation from Oxford, but was turned down.) The more personal attack on Arnold can be seen in comments that regard education as a ghastly imposition:

> If you meet at dinner a man who has spent his life in educating himself – a rare type in our time, I admit, but still one occasionally to be met with – you rise from table richer and conscious that a high ideal has for a moment touched and sanctified your days. But oh! my dear Ernest, to sit next a man who has spent his life in trying to educate others! What a dreadful experience that is! How appalling is that ignorance which is the inevitable result of the fatal habit of imparting opinions! . . . People say that the schoolmaster is abroad. I wish to goodness he were.

(CW: 1140)

This is quite funny, but it is at least a bit unkind to a figure who had been significant in Wilde's own intellectual development and who was very recently dead.

The key element of 'The Critic as Artist' is one of the anxieties that all critics share – Ernest asks us to consider the popular contention that criticism is not really worthwhile, being a much lesser occupation than creative production; Gilbert argues forcefully against the binary hierarchy constructed by his friend, who has borrowed some of Arnold's critical clothes to become Gilbert's 'Aunt Sally'. Rejecting Ernest's view of the dichotomy between creativity and criticism, he says;

> The antithesis between them is entirely arbitrary. Without the critical faculty, there is no artistic creation at all, worthy of the name. You spoke . . . of that fine spirit of choice and delicate instinct of selection by which the artist realises life for us, and give to it a momentary perfection. Well, the spirit of choice, that subtle tact of omission, is really the critical faculty in . . . and no one who does not possess this critical faculty can create anything at all in art. Arnold's definition of literature as a criticism of life was not very felicitous in form, but showed how keenly he recognised the importance of the critical element in all creative work.
>
> (CW: 1118)

At this stage of the argument, Gilbert has remained within the bounds of what most people would consider as reasonable, and within the terms of Arnold's original argument about the necessity of criticism. The creative artist is his/her own greatest critic; the creative process involves the rejection of unsuitable forms and it is the critic inside the artist who knows what must be rejected. But Gilbert, like Wilde himself, does not confine himself to the merely reasonable. He claims further that the critic who is not the artist has the same, if not greater, importance for art as a whole as the critic inside the artist. So when the agonized Ernest (whose name contains that sense of straightforward honesty, which is sent up repeatedly in Wilde's work) asks if Gilbert really believes that criticism is a creative art, we are not surprised to hear Gilbert say: 'Why should it not be? It works with materials and puts them into a form that is at once new and delightful. What more can one say of poetry? Indeed, I would call criticism a creation within a creation' (CW: 1125).

From this point on Wilde channels Walter Pater, with his sense that criticism operates to demonstrate the sensitive personality of the critic, and that particular acts of interpretation depend not on some objective notion of reality (the object as in itself it really is, as Arnold would say), but rather on the critic creating insights out of his own temperament. Gilbert actually quotes verbatim Pater's most famous critical passage, his description of the *Mona Lisa*, commenting in the preface, 'Who . . . cares whether Mr. Pater has put into the portrait of the Mona Lisa something that Leonardo never dreamed of?' (CW: 1126), and concluding:

> the criticism which I have quoted is criticism of the highest kind. It treats the work art simply as a starting point for a new creation. It does not confine itself . . . to discovering the real intention of the artist and accepting that as final. . . . the meaning of any beautiful created thing is at least as much in the soul of him who looks at it, as it was in his soul who wrought it. . . . when the work has finished, it has . . . an independent . . . and may deliver a message far other than that which was put into its lips to say.

What Gilbert, as a critic, and perhaps Wilde as an artist, both reject is any kind of art that has only one message, which can be fixed or final; indeed, if it has only one message, then it isn't art – 'a truth in art is that whose contradictory is also true', as he put it at the end of 'The Truth of Masks' (CW: 1173). What is to be preferred are artistic productions that are deliberately uncertain or vague, such as the painting of the impressionists, and particularly music. Pater had said in *The Renaissance* that 'all art constantly aspires to the condition of music' (Pater 1980: 106), meaning that the ideal art was one in which form and content could not be separated. Gilbert picks up Pater's preferences, and indeed vocabulary, and recycles them ('Pen, Pencil and Poison' is subtitled 'A Study in Green': it might have been an equally useful subtitle for the two dialogues as well).

> The aesthetic critic rejects those obvious modes of art that have but one message to deliver, and having delivered it become dumb and sterile, and seeks rather for such modes as suggest reverie and mood, and by their imaginative beauty make all interpretations true, and no interpretation final'.
>
> (CW: 1129)

As in 'The Decay of Lying', where the making of art is made dependent on personality, so in 'The Critic as Artist' II, criticism and interpretation are also based on it. 'Art springs from personality,' says Gilbert, 'so it is only to personality that it can be revealed, and from the meaning comes right interpretative criticism.'

Ernest tries to persuade Gilbert that the critic should be rational, fair and sincere; these are the terms of reason, the privileged terms in the binary hierarchy, and also the Arnoldian criticism, slightly recast. Gilbert rejects them all. Fairness (objectivity or 'disinterestedness') and sincerity are rejected because they confuse morality with art: 'the first condition of criticism is that the critic should be able to recognise that the sphere of art and the sphere of ethics are absolutely distinct and separate.' And the rational is rejected as a criterion for judgement because the aim of art, Gilbert has earlier suggested is 'simply to create a mood', which is presumably something to which rationality cannot be expected to apply. It is temperament that is seen by Gilbert as the primary requisite of the critic. And it is form rather than substance (style, not sincerity, as Wilde put it elsewhere) to which the critic should pay attention:

> In every sphere of life, form is the beginning of things. . . . Forms are the food of faith. . . . The Creeds are believed not because they are rational, but because they are repeated. Yes: Form is everything.
> (CW: 1148–9)

This is a shocking statement, which would have appeared profane to many original readers. The creeds, the central statements of Christian belief are powerful, not because they are rational/logical, but because they have a repetitive structure, and are repeated each week in the churches. Our response to them is an emotional response to their *forms*, not a logical response to their *content*. Thus, all the models by which society thinks that the world is constructed, are each considered in turn, and rejected by Gilbert first because they are irrational, and secondly because they are unbeautiful.

Both the discussion of form and the embodiment of form are part of the reason I wanted to consider these pieces of philosophical art criticism in the light of Wilde's other works. One of the things that they both do rather successfully is to blur the distinctions between art and life and art and criticism, not in their content, but in their forms (and form is everything), disrupting generic convention. What Wilde has done is to create characters who can speak arguments, pretty much like characters in a play. There is no explicit interference from the writer himself. In choosing this form, Wilde was referring back to the traditions of Greek philosophy, and in particular to the so-called Socratic method of argument in which the teacher (Socrates), rather than lecturing his 'pupils', draws out their views by asking them intelligent and loaded questions. The implicit reference to the Socratic dialogue in the form of the pieces is important to Wilde because it at once confers respectability – Socrates and Plato are the two founding fathers of Western philosophy and culture – and yet also simultaneously hints at the moral dubiousness of same-sex desire. Wilde uses the genre of the Socratic dialogue and reverses the direction of learning by having the questioner play the role of the naïve or ingenuous pupil in need of instruction. The traffic between disciple and prophet is not only one way. And for the reader 'in the know', classically educated, for instance, the lessons of the dialogue operate within a context that is at least homosocial, and may also be homoerotic: The dialogue is a playful and even seductive form. In both cases, the two sets of young men stay up all night discussing these things – like lovers perhaps. Manly young men with economically productive jobs and beautiful wives should be in bed asleep, a trope that is repeated in the seduction of Dorian Gray by Lord Henry Wootton. Moreover, in both cases the young man who is to be persuaded is not persuaded by rational argument so much as by the sheer intoxication of words: Gilbert, for example, wins the argument by lyrical examples, rather than by logical ones, reeling off long lists of things that may be only very tangentially relevant; Ernest is 'seduced' rather than convinced into agreement. The dialogue form, then, has several advantages from Wilde's point of view. For one thing, the rather outrageous views that the essays expound are not presented as his own, but as those of fictional characters. For another, the dialogue form allows him to put across more than one contradictory point of view, and to express views with which he did not agree in order to refute them. There is a double reading/meaning at least possible from the form the dialogues take.

By putting what we assume are his own views into the mouth of a character, Wilde is calling into question the status of what we are reading; this is a two-faced art, rather than a totalizing position – and it is up to the reader to decide where they stand in relation to it. The text itself refuses to give us clear answers. In general terms, however, we can see Wilde arguing that art is not moral, not didactic, not objective – he takes Pater's part against Arnold and Ruskin; but he states Pater's position much more forcefully and unsubtly than Pater himself ever would have done, courting the dangers that his teacher merely skirted.

Material World and the Socialist Soul

In a great deal of Wilde's writing there is a concern with the materiality of existence. As we shall see in the next chapter, it is a significant issue in some of the short stories, particularly the fairy stories, such as 'The Happy Prince' and 'The Young King' where the luxuries of the privileged are shown to be absolutely based on the material lack and the extraction of surplus value from the very poor. Fairy stories, being what they are, do not offer political solutions to these problems, except inasmuch as the individual benevolence of Prince and King is able to solve them (and both these solutions are extremely limited). But the genre of an essay entitled 'The Soul of Man under Socialism' might well be expected to do precisely that – to explain how the diagnosis of social ills might be turned to cure. However, this is Wilde we are talking about, and 'The Soul of Man' inhabits exactly the same camp reversal of values and refusal of 'usefulness' that can be seen in the other substantial essays. This is only very loosely an essay about socialism as generally understood, signalled from its very title: this is an essay that values the soul (immaterial, essence, immanence) in a discourse that is supposed to be materialist and that stresses the importance of individualism in a supposedly communal or social system. In these emphases, the essay is almost consistent with Wilde's other works, but it is clearly not consistent with socialism.

The essay, first published in the *Fortnightly Review* in 1891, does define socialism in ways that are congruent with other contemporary definitions, for example, that published by Eleanor Marx and Edward Aveling in their privately printed *Shelley's Socialism* (1888), in which they listed six propositions of what socialism meant 'to some of us':

(1) That there are inequality and misery in the world; (2) that this social inequality . . . [is] the necessary outcome of our social conditions; (3) that the essence of these social conditions is that the mass of the people . . . produce and distribute all commodities, while a minority of the people . . . possess these commodities; (4) that this initial tyranny of the possessing class over the producing class is based on the present wage system and now maintains all other forms of oppression, such as that of monarchy, or clerical rule, or police despotism; (5) that this tyranny of the few over the many is only possible because the few have obtained . . . all the means of

> production and distribution of commodities . . . (6) . . . that the
> approaching change in civilized society will be a revolution . . . The
> two classes . . . will be replaced by a single class consisting of the whole
> of the healthy and sane members of the community possessing all the
> means of production and distribution in common.
>
> (Thompson 1977: 331–2)

Each of these propositions is repeated by Wilde, though in a different style. He begins with the statement that 'Socialism would relieve us of the sordid necessity of living for others', a necessity that arises from the inequalities and miseries of the poor. The need for revolution, then, comes from the miserable conditions of poverty, but more particularly from the effects of those conditions on the rich. Where he differs from a more traditional notion of socialism's focus is that his emphasis is on the aesthetic effects – the ugliness – of poverty, on rich and poor alike, rather than on the material effects of poverty on the poor. There is no economic analysis of the actual processes of manufacture and distribution of commodities; but there is an analysis of the *effects* of those systems. One of the effects is the charity of the rich who feel guilty about their privilege, and end up spoiling their lives 'by an unhealthy and exaggerated altruism'. This emphasis is wrong, Wilde argues. Rather than trying to keep the poor alive by individual acts of charity, or in the case of a 'very advanced school', trying to 'amuse the poor', the proper aim of life is 'to reconstruct society on such a basis that poverty will be impossible.' 'Charity,' he writes, 'creates a multitude of sins' because it is 'immoral to use private property to alleviate the horrible evils that result from the institution of private property' (CW: 1174). The system itself needs to be reformed, though the process of reformation or revolution is never described.

Wilde's views on charity appear, at first sight, to be extreme and strange, even as they are also characteristically witty, but in fact, as I have suggested elsewhere (Robbins 2000: 99–112), there had been a debate about the effects of individual benevolence in the pages of journals such as *The Fortnightly* in which 'Soul' appeared. The tenor of these debates was a version of social Darwinism, in that charity was felt to be a means to ensuring that the 'unfittest' survived, and that therefore charity was 'against nature' in some way. Wilde's wit is actually considerably less disturbing and rather more humane (if not very practical) than the views propounded by some writers that the poor should be allowed to go to the dogs in their own way.

The importance of socialism, Wilde argued, is that it will lead necessarily to individualism, an interestingly and paradoxically bourgeois notion of selfhood in this context. At the moment, the poor can have no individualism, since they are so degraded into a mass that they are scarcely even conscious of their own suffering: 'They have to be told of it by other people, and they often entirely disbelieve them.' (CW: 1176) But the real problems of private property rebound most of all on those who own it. Private property exacts duties from its owners, and prevents them from realising their own individuality:

> private property has really harmed Individualism, and obscured it, by confusing a man with what he possesses . . . man thought that the important thing was to have, and did not know that the important thing is to be. The true perfection of man lies, not in what man has, but in what man is.
>
> (CW: 1178)

In other words, both the ownership of property and the lack of it produce slavish conformity to externally imposed standards that a given subject has not chosen or made. Wilde sees conformity as the most serious threat to the individual because it insists on an 'absolute uniformity of type' (CW: 1195). This is another version of his adherence to Pater's principle that 'our failure is to form habits'. The loss of individualism makes art impossible since true art, and the true artist, are never conformist. And the existence of art and artists is the proper measure of the quality of any society, since the artist is the supreme individualist who can only thrive if there is no authoritarian government that enforces any kind of conformity.

Wilde implicitly defines the goal of socialism as being the social organization that allows everyone to live with the freedoms of an artist; in other words, he suggests that life and art need to come together across both aesthetic and social boundaries. All the current systems of government destroy the conditions necessary to the existence of the supreme individualist, the artist:

> all authority is equally bad. There are three kinds of despots. There is the despot who tyrannises over the body. There is the despot who tyrannises over the soul. There is the despot who tyrannises over the

soul and body alike. The first is called the Prince. The second is called the Pope. The third is called the People.

(CW: 1193)

All three systems – monarchy, ecclesiastical rule and democracy – enforce conformity, and mistake conformity for morality, a point that develops one also made in 'The Critic as Artist' (1891), where Gilbert tells Ernest: 'The security of society lies in custom and unconscious instinct . . . the basis of the stability of society' (CW: 1141).

The tone of Wilde's arguments in all his writings depends crucially on his sense of audience and on his own (constructed) subject position in relation to the audience he constructs as his (implied) readership as we saw above. As Regenia Gagnier argues, his prose writings display both cynicism and idealism, with cynicism producing his character-istic wit and distance, and his idealism, the seduction of his purple prose: 'This doubleness constituted Wilde's response to the modern bourgeois artist's dilemma between private art and the need for an audience' (Gagnier 1986: 19). In 'Pen, Pencil and Poison: A Study in Green', Wilde used the assumptions of the essay genre against them-selves. The implied (male) audience of like-minded proper gentlemen was comically coerced – seduced almost, one might say – into assent-ing to the essay's outrageous propositions. That essay, like 'The Soul of Man', exemplifies Wilde's strategy of using dominant discourses, in particular the vocabulary and assumptions of conformist masculinity against the very assumptions of that discourse, through a tone that resists the certainties that the vocabulary would usually imply. So, in 'The Soul of Man' we read:

> The possession of private property is very often extremely demoralising and that is, of course, why Socialism wants to get rid of the institution . . . Some years ago people went about the country saying that property has duties . . . at last, the Church has begun to say it. One hears it now from every pulpit. It is perfectly true. Property not merely has duties, it has so many duties that its possession to any large extent is a bore. It involves endless claims upon one, endless attention to business, endless bother. If property had simply pleasures, we could stand it; but its duties make it unbearable. In the interest of the rich we must get rid of it.

(CW: 1175–6)

Wilde's point requires the existence of the language of *noblesse oblige* (a phrase meaning that the upper classes are obliged to help the poor because of the privilege of their own position); it requires also the Church's discourse of altruism and the Christian denial of earthly pleasures in the expectation of heavenly reward; further, in a different version of the joke in *The Importance of Being Earnest*, it requires the punning meaning of 'duties' meaning 'taxation' (as in death duties). As Lady Bracknell puts it, 'with the duties expected of one during one's lifetime and the duties exacted from one after one's death', property-ownership 'has ceased to be either a profit or a pleasure' (CW: 368). The joke depends on the existence of commonly held beliefs that are then subverted into apparent paradoxes such as getting rid of property to benefit the rich. But while the audience may laugh, it will probably not be converted, which – generically at least – really ought to be the aim of an essay on socialism.

In relation to the question of individualism, the technique is slightly different. In this case, Wilde takes standard contemporary ideas about individualism and, instead of reversing the discourse, he pushes the concept to its logical limits, demonstrating in the process that individualism, as understood by the nineteenth century, is always already a paradox. As Raymond Williams observes in *Keywords*: 'Individual originally meant indivisible. That now sounds like a paradox. "Individual" stresses a distinction from others; "indivisible" a necessary connection' (Williams 1988: 161). Williams shows us that 'individualism' is a nineteenth-century coinage, which draws on the idea of the individual as a 'unique person' who also has 'his [*sic*] (indivisible) membership of a group.' Individualism makes use of both uniqueness and group membership, and argues for the primacy of the individual's own interests over the interests of the group (1988: 162). On the one hand, then, individualism is bound up with ideas about the uniqueness, self-expressiveness, internal coherence and originality of proper masculinity.

In this model, individualism is not a conformist doctrine, but one that demands originality – non-conformity – as its goal and method. At the same time, however, acceptable individualism also depended on a degree of self-abnegation and conformity. Restraint and reserve imply that the individual is not to draw attention to himself, and yet he must always behave as if he were being observed. As James Eli Adams suggests, 'the masculine, in short, is as much a spectacle as the feminine' (Adams 1995: 11). Masculine individualism is caught up in the paradox of the necessary display of virtue (which is most usually to be understood as conformity to pre-existing moral values) and the necessity not to stand out from the crowd: the Victorian individual is both an aesthete and an ascetic.

The Wildean individual, on the other hand, focuses on his own originality and abandons restraint, taking Mill at his word. The effect is powerful because his implied audience is a homosocial coterie of men – and 'artistic' men at that; men, that is who are *au fait* with contemporary discourses of masculinity, but who are prepared to divorce themselves from the capitalist and heterosexual modes of production and reproduction sanctioned by dominant versions of individualism. As Lawrence Danson has noted, individualism could mean anything from the very negative view of it as 'individual isolation and social dissolution' to the very positive, which emphasised 'the organic unity of individual and society' (Danson 1997: 161–2). Wilde's individualism, as always, refuses the hierarchical valuation of that neat binary of positive and negative: dissolution of the current social order presumably is precisely what socialism aims at, and organic unity is thus itself dissolved as a valued term that can have no positive meaning while it still attaches itself to the status quo.

In other words, 'The Soul of Man' is a text which, from its very title, operates on deliberate mis-recognitions (themselves dependent on careful recognitions) of contemporary language codes. The earnestness of contemporary versions of masculinity is invoked only to be debunked. Similarly, the earnestness of contemporary socialist writing, the commonplace attitudes of the activists, is also mocked: in this text, labour is not dignified but disgusting; poverty is ugly rather than immoral; property demoralises the rich; socialism is not communal. Wilde combines two kinds of knowing joke, against masculinity and against socialism in his essay. But these are jokes told from a position of constructed privilege. It would be difficult to make the joke, and impossible to find it funny, if you lived in real poverty. This does not mean that the joke is unimportant, but it has more to say about Man than Socialism, and it explicitly refuses the realm of the practical in its rhetorical strategies, its subject matter, its implied writer and his implied audience.

In the end, Wilde's socialism is a theoretical intervention. As he says himself near the end of the 'The Soul of Man', his ideas about socialism will be attacked as unpractical and as going against human nature:

> This is perfectly true. It is unpractical, and it goes against human nature. This is why it is worth carrying out, and that is why one proposes it. For what is a practical scheme? A practical scheme is either a scheme that is already in existence, or a scheme that could be carried out under existing conditions. But it is exactly the existing conditions that one objects to; and any scheme that could accept these conditions is wrong and foolish. The conditions will be done away with, and human nature will change.
>
> (CW: 1194)

Wilde has nothing to offer in terms of describing *how* socialism will be achieved, concentrating all his attention on why it should be achieved. He proposes ideal ends, but proposes no means – no practice that will make the theory come true. How could there be action? As others of Wilde's critical writings show, ethics and aesthetics have no relation to each other. The relationships between world and word are tenuous and fleeting. Anyone acting on them is obviously behaving absurdly, for criticism and commitment do not belong in the same sentence.

Chapter Three
Prose: Short Fictional

Fairy Tales

In a discussion of Wilde's fairy stories in *Oscar Wilde: Works of a Conformist Rebel*, Norbert Kohl argues that 'in form and structure, Wilde's fairytales are very much in the tradition of European folktales. The characters are one-dimensional, without psychological motivation . . . they are simply the nameless bearers of particular qualities and functions' (Kohl 1989: 55). Kohl's discussion suggests that Wilde's adherence to the generic structure established by traditional European folktales is a severe limitation on their aesthetic potency. He is concerned by their lack of 'social or historical setting', of psychological complexity and realistic development in characters, and in the elaboration of the action. To quite a great extent, those comments are fair, though the disappointed tone of Kohl's critique perhaps is not. The implicit judgement he makes is that the stories are failures in some sense because they do not dramatize action, personality and event in the terms of realist fiction, with its emphases on a solidly realized world, where rounded characters live and learn from their experiences. Wilde, it would appear, in this discussion, sticks to the generic limitations of the fairy story and is judged wanting because he has not written another kind of fiction. My view is slightly different. While elements of Kohl's remarks are clearly correct, I want to suggest that the fairy stories are not exactly generically stable; and that their 'message' might equally be read as more unsettling than the fairy-story world would usually imply, not least because they are 'seductive' fictions, often focused on a luxurious material world that offers repeated opportunities for Wilde, the author, to indulge in what

Kohl calls his 'predilection for lavish décor' (1989: 56). There are implications to that predilection that do not belong in the allegedly innocent world of 'faerie'.

In Wilde's two collections of fairy stories, *The Happy Prince and Other Stories* (published by David Nutt in 1888) and *A House of Pomegranates* (Osgood McIlvaine, 1891), the oral Wilde discussed briefly above in Chapter 2 takes on a different guise. As Jerusha McCormack puts it, 'Wilde's shorter fictions are oral in origin and are written as performances' (McCormack 1997: 102). The fairy story, which derives from the oral folktale, draws on the oral elements that were once part of what Walter J. Ong describes as the process of transmitting 'hard-won' knowledge, which the narrative was meant to impart. In primary oral cultures, he writes, 'to solve effectively the problem of retaining and retrieving carefully articulated thought, you have to do your thinking in mnemonic patterns, shaped ready for oral recurrence' (Ong 1982: 34). In its oral form, the formulaic elements of 'once upon a time', 'happily ever after', the repetitive elements, usually focused on the number three (three wishes, three attempts at a particular task, three gifts, three little pigs, three dreams, as in 'The Young King') enforce the practical wisdom that the tale was originally meant to deliver. As folk tale morphed into fairy story (fairy story is the literary inheritor of the earlier oral form) the practical wisdom became less significant than the morality of the tale, but the ghosts of the recurrent structures, which reinforced the message of the story from earlier times, still haunt the literary version of the mode. As Wilde was to comment satirically elsewhere, on the Victorian novel, in the fairy story 'the good ended happily and the bad ended unhappily. That is what fiction means' (CW: 376). The black and white identification of good and bad was supposed to be simple; and the narrative trajectory made absolutely clear that good would triumph. As a narrative form meant for simple folk and thence for children, the fairy story was meant to be a very easily legible lesson: legible in both senses in that its language (vocabulary and grammatical structure) is usually pared down and its message is clear. However, as we read Wilde's fairy stories, we are struck by the fact that they are not quite so simple as the generic rules would imply. The stories seem to say complex things when we expect a child's story to simplify for the sake of the child; and they say those things in a complex way, using a vocabulary, sentence structure and tone that are beyond the technical reading ability and the understanding of the 'average British' child (whoever that is: Wilde explicitly disavowed the average British child as his intended audience, as we shall see). While the world that his stories inhabit is clearly the world of the fairy tale (a never-never land of once-upon-a-time and make-believe), which pushes towards the interpretation that the stories are for children (Victorian adults, of course, have to remain strictly within the realms of the real, and within the conventions of realism), they are too complex on all levels for any reader to be quite sure.

It is possible that Wilde was influenced by his Irish heritage in his choice of the fairy-tale genre, and McCormack certainly thinks that this is the case, arguing briefly that Irish nationalism via the attempt to promote a resurgence in Irish national culture was at the heart of Wilde's project (McCormack 1997: 102). Both Sir William and Lady Wilde had collected folk-tales and legends from the Irish peasantry. And both Wilde's parents had published collections of these stories: Sir William's *Irish Popular Superstitions* came out in 1852; and Lady Wilde's *Ancient Legends: Mystic Charms and Superstitions of Ireland* (based in part on her late husband's research) was published, to great acclaim, in 1887. The attraction of the fairy story as a genre is multiple. It offers a genre that is apparently innocent (because of its implied audience), but which may yet contain hidden messages. It is able to do this because it resists realism, the dominant mode of prose narrative throughout the nineteenth century. In his essay 'The Decay of Lying', a very direct attack on realism as we have seen, Wilde had written: 'if something cannot be done to check, or at least modify, our monstrous worship of facts, Art will become sterile and beauty will pass away from the land' (CW: 1074). And he concludes that essay with the statement: 'the telling of beautiful untrue things is the proper aim of art' (CW: 1091–2). Realism is, above all, a discourse of authority, which reinforces the claims of dominant groups to rule; it is often the language of colonialism and imperialism and the shift away from its authority can be understood as a shift away from the politics of power it represents. One of the reasons Wilde may have chosen to retreat from 'reality' into the realm of myth and faerie, is that it is one place in which they are able to express an alternative version of the real, which undermines that presented by colonising English, or the hegemonic virtues of straight-talking (heterosexual) masculinity. Realism claims to represent the real, apparently in an unmediated way.

In its focus on reality – on things as they are – it prevents the reader and writer from imagining alternative realities, alternative ways of understanding the world and living within it. Indeed, Lady Wilde, in a passage from the introduction to her *Ancient Legends*, wrote:

> Dogmatic religion and science have long since killed the mythopoetic faculty in cultured Europe. It only exists now, naturally and instinctively, in children, poets, and the childlike races, like the Irish – simple, joyous, reverent and unlettered, and who have remained unchanged for centuries, walled round by their language from the rest of Europe, through which separating veil, science, culture and the cold mockery of the sceptic have never yet penetrated.
>
> (Cohen 1978: 75)

There is obviously a problem with seeing the Irish as a 'childlike' race – that could even be the language of the colonizer rather than of their nationalist defender; but the point here is that such a construction of a nation as childlike and simple also offers a position from which to attack the reality/realism, which constructed the Irish a subaltern group within the realm of the British empire. In Speranza's terms, the Irish might be childlike, but they are also poetic, which gives them an alternative form of power to political power; the combination of political subordination with bardic insubordination, one might say. If one chooses to read them along these lines, the stories of *The Happy Prince* and *The House of Pomegranates* can be seen to have something of a political edge to them in a veiled Irish nationalist message, though this is a bit of an interpretative stretch. Clearer is the 'socialistic' message that one reviewer noted as being part of the later volume. And it is also possible to see them, in McCormack's terms, as 'fairy stories' of a different kind – drawing on a slang usage of the word fairy that was coming into being towards the end of the nineteenth century, to signify male effeminacy and/or same-sex desire.

All of this means that the implied audience for Wilde's tales is a complex business. As Guy and Small (2000) point out, the actual physical appearances of the two volumes of stories suggested differing audiences. *The Happy Prince* possibly really was a children's book; *A House of Pomegranates*, in a limited and very expensive deluxe edition, by contrast was clearly a collector's item, aimed at a small, select, even coterie audience. This confusion about the audience for the stories, which is, of course also a question of genre, was registered in some of the contemporary reviews. Alexander Galt Ross (elder brother of Wilde's devoted friend Robert Ross) writing the *Saturday Review* in October 1888 about *The Happy Prince*, commented:

> One of the chief functions of the true fairy story is to excite sympathy. Whether they are princes, peasants, or inanimate objects . . . the joys and sorrows of the heroes and heroines of fairyland will always be real to those persons, whatever their age may be, who love the fairy story, and regard it as the most excellent form of romance. Mr. Oscar Wilde, no doubt for the most excellent reasons, has chosen to present his fables in the form of fairy tales to *a public which . . . will assuredly not be composed of children*. No child will sympathize at all with Mr. Wilde's *Happy Prince* when he melted down by order of the Mayor and Corporation . . . Children do not care for satire, and the dominant spirit of these stories is satire – a bitter satire.
>
> (CH: 61, my emphasis)

This says quite a lot about what adults regard as suitable reading for children, and speaks to a construction of innocence in childhood that is particularly 'Victorian'; the teaching of appropriate emotions, such as 'sympathy' for instance, is about both children's emotional needs and about a view of the appropriate functions of the literary text. The same criticism (that the stories are not meant for children at all) in a different, and more hostile, form arose again when the second volume of stories was published two years later. The anonymous reviewer for the *Pall Mall Gazette* (30 November 1891) wrote of *A House of Pomegranates*:

> Is *A House of Pomegranates* intended for a child's book? We confess that we do not exactly know. The ultra-aestheticism of the pictures seems unsuitable for children – as also the rather 'fleshly' style of Mr. Wilde's writing . . . Mr. Wilde's diction seems to us hardly suitable for children. Joys are 'fierce' and 'fiery-coloured'; the King, watching his little daughter at play, thinks of her dead and embalmed mother and . . . 'the odours of strange spices, spices such as embalmers use, seemed to taint – or was it fancy? – the clear morning air.'
>
> (CH: 113–4)

The 'sympathy' that Galt Ross identified as essential to writing for children certainly does not extend to the possibility that emotions may be sensualized or even sexualized in children's books. This commentary, which also contained reference to the 'scandal' of *Dorian Gray,* which had also just been published in volume form, provoked Wilde, more than once. Not only did he respond to it in 'The Critic as Artist' as we have seen (in Chapter 2), but he also wrote to the *Pall Mall*'s editor to defend his stories and to state quite publicly that they were not children's stories at all:

> Sir, I have just had sent to me from London a copy of the *Pall Mall Gazette* containing a review of my book *A House of Pomegranates*. The writer of this review makes a certain suggestion about my book which I beg you will allow me to correct at once.
>
> He starts by asking an extremely silly question, and that is, whether or not I have written this book for the purpose of giving pleasure to the British child. Having expressed grave doubts on this subject, a subject on which I cannot conceive any fairly educated person having any doubts at all, he proceeds, apparently quite seriously, to make the extremely limited vocabulary at the disposal of the British child the standard by which the prose of an artist is to be judged! Now in building this *House of Pomegranates* I had about as much intention of pleasing the British child as I had of pleasing the British public. . . . No artist recognises any standard of beauty but that which is suggested by his own temperament.
>
> (CL: 503)

This is a fairly disingenuous defence. Wilde muddied the waters about the intended audience for the two volumes. Sometimes he claimed they were written for his own children (though when they were first published, Cyril and Vyvyan would certainly have been too young to have been able to read them for themselves, and possibly too young to have had them read aloud to them). On other occasions, he suggested that childlike people as opposed to actual children were his audience. Writing to one correspondent with a copy of *The Happy Prince* as a gift, he said: the tales were 'meant partly for children, and partly for those who have kept the childlike faculties of wonder and joy, and who find in simplicity a subtle strangeness' (CL: 352). And to Amelie

Rives Chanler, he wrote in 1889, that they were: 'an attempt to mirror modern life in a form remote from reality – to deal with modern problems in a mode that is ideal and not imitative. . . . they are, of course, slight and fanciful, and written not for children, but for the childlike people from eighteen to eighty' (CL: 388). In his comments he iterates his dislike of realism, but he does not entirely settle on a readership that would make the generic status of his stories clear.

In fact, although both volumes are fairy stories, they are probably addressed to different audiences, with *The Happy Prince* containing more that is childlike, and *The House of Pomegranates* certainly implying a more adult audience. The second volume in particular has a vocabulary and style that is very complex, and produces stories that are antipathetic to the traditional fairy-tale because of their return to the real as opposed to the perpetuation of a world of 'happily ever after'. For example, the dwarf in 'The Birthday of the Infanta' dies at the end – the genre does not rescue him to a happy ending produced out of magic, and it does not redeem the self-absorption of the Infanta who does not even recognize the pathos of the dwarf's death: 'For the future let those who come to play with me have no hearts,' is her only comment on his demise (CW: 235). Similarly 'The Star Child' does not live happily ever after, redeemed by suffering, but dies because of his suffering, and his kingdom is 'ruled evilly' by 'he who came after'. And in 'The Fisherman and his Soul', despite the miraculous growth of flowers on the graves of the fisherman and the mermaid, there is no reconciliation between Christian and pagan values, represented by the priest, and the seafolk who leave the bay behind. In contrast, *The Happy Prince* remains closer to the functions of the traditional folk-tale genre.

The title story of the first of Wilde's volumes picks up on two themes that are central to his later work – the relationship of life and art, particularly as it is focused through (adolescent) male beauty, and the disjunction between appearance and reality. The first theme takes off from the central fact of the story, that the statue of the happy prince is animate: this is a life that is also a work of art, a trope we have already seen played out in very different contexts in 'Charmides' and *The Sphinx* and which is also central to 'The Portrait of Mr W. H.' and *The Picture of Dorian Gray* as Chapter 4 will show. The statue is clearly an artwork in Wilde's estimation because it is read so differently by different people, following the view expressed in 'The

Truth of Masks': 'A truth in art is that whose contradictory is also true' (CW: 1173); the statue of the happy prince produces suitably contradictory responses. The town council see it as a reflection of their own glory and political prestige. A 'sensible mother' regards him as a moral lesson to her own child: 'Why can't you be like the Happy Prince? . . . The Happy Prince never dreams of crying for anything' (CW: 271). A philosopher looks at him as an image of impossible happiness. And the charity children regard him as an angel, food for their imaginations if not for their stomachs. That is, the prince is an image at once of reality (the political and ideological views represented by politicians and unimaginative mothers) and romance (the imaginations of the charity children). The second theme of the story, the disjunction between appearance and reality, takes off from the fact that this beautifully rich statue entitled the Happy Prince is in fact not happy at all, expressed pithily in the first exchange between the statue and the swallow: the swallow asks who the statue is: '"I am the Happy Prince." "Why are you weeping then?" asked the swallow' (CW: 272). The sensible mother is proven wrong by the fact that the swallow has been soaked almost to drowning by the tears of a prince who apparently never cries for anything, but in reality is weeping for all the woes of the world.

The way that the story is constructed depends on the reader's acceptance of several impossibilities – that a statue can speak to a swallow; that the swallow can speak back, though these impossibilities are standard elements of the fairy-story genre and of what Freud regarded as the natural animism of children, that is, their capacity to imbue inanimate objects with life. The more literal minded of Wilde's reviewers, like the charity-schoolmaster in the story, who 'did not approve of children dreaming' (CW: 207), objected to Wilde's evocation of the child's fantastic reality. The childlike qualities of the story, then, have to do with both the acceptance of the impossible and the teaching of a specific moral value: that where people are in pain or need, it is the moral obligation of others to relieve that suffering. On that level it is a simple moral tale. The statue is stripped of its precious gilding and stone in order to relieve the poverty of those in the prince's city, with the result that 'the children's faces grew rosier, and they laughed and played in the street. "We have bread now," they cried' (CW: 276). But the extent to which the prince's charity has any lasting result is a moot point in the story; the children may be fed for now, which is clearly important, but the status quo of the ruling body remains in place, and there may not be jam tomorrow. The mayor and corporation have no recognition of what has happened. They merely see the stripped down statue as a poor reflection of their political importance. The fact that they are still the rulers at the end implies that the sacrifices of prince and swallow have brought about no change in the world itself. The individual acts of charity, while they relieve individual cases of need, do not fundamentally alter the system that perpetuates that need. The story scarcely asks or answers the question of why people live in poverty. There is just the merest hint of the structural relationship between the rich and the poor in the vignette of the prince's first act of charity towards a seamstress with a sick child.

> 'Far away,' continued the statue in a low musical voice, 'far away in a little street, there is a poor house. One of the windows is open, and through it I can see a woman seated at a table. Her face is thin and worn, and she has coarse red hands, all pricked by the needle, for she is a seamstress. She is embroidering passion-flowers on a satin gown for the loveliest of the Queen's maids-of-honour to wear at the next Court-ball. In a bed in the corner of the room her little boy is lying ill. He has a fever, and is asking for oranges. His mother has nothing to give him but river water, so he is crying. Swallow, Swallow, little Swallow, will you not bring her the ruby out of my sword-hilt?'
>
> (CW: 272–3)

On his way to the seamstress the swallow passes the balcony of the woman for whom the dress is being made: 'I hope my dress will be ready in time for the State-ball,' she says. 'I have ordered passion-flowers to be embroidered on it, but the seamstresses are so lazy.' (CW: 272) No comment is made on this beyond the one that is made by simple juxtaposition; the reader is left to draw his/her own conclusions about the problem of a capitalist economy, and some readers may choose to draw no lesson at all at that level, focusing on the story's emphasis on individual good works.

However, when one compares 'The Happy Prince' to 'The Young King' in the later volume, it becomes apparent that the earlier volume is more childlike than the second precisely because it does not raise these issues in a more politically charged manner. At the end of 'The Happy Prince' nothing has changed. This is a case in which one swallow does not a summer make. The politicians of the corporation merely argue about which of them should replace the prince in effigy. The value of what the prince has done is beyond worldly appreciation. Only God, sending down his ministering angel, knows that the two most valuable things in city are the prince's leaden heart and the swallow's body. And in all the stories of the collection except for 'The Remarkable Rocket', we are shown, not only that self-sacrifice is worthy, but also that it is never valued properly, and that it may in fact be pointless. The nightingale, who sings out her heart's blood for a red rose has made a useless sacrifice; Hans, the devoted friend, is hideously exploited by the miller who has a marvellous rhetoric of friendship, but none of its actual attributes – appearance and reality yet again do not match; the selfish giant learns to share his possessions – and then he dies. He may very well go to heaven; but the promise of happily-ever-after that is not in the here-and-now is a particular problem for the morality that is supposed to be the bread-and-butter of this genre of tale.

In the later volume, 'The Young King' takes up a similar theme, to 'The Happy Prince'. Both stories are about the evils of current social organization. But whereas the happy prince attempts to solve those problems only by looking at the individual cases of those who suffer and acting individually to solve them, at least in the short term, the young king is forced to think through the structural relationships between poverty and riches. It is a story about the means of production and their implications. It also typifies the *House of Pomegranates* volume in that it is written in a very lush style: in the words of Anne Varty, in this volume,

> Wilde was writing to please himself . . . the prose style of each tale is an exercise in artificial display. Composition, mood, and tone are foregrounded by archaic sentence structure, specialised diction and a deliberate patterning of adventure, forcing storyline and moral into positions of secondary importance.
>
> (Varty 1998: 97)

Similarly McCormack describes the style of 'The Fisherman and his Soul' as 'Asiatic: jewelled, ornamented, heavily allusive to the exotic allure of the East' (McCormack 1997: 103), comments that also apply to the prose of 'The Young King', which offers a wealth of detail, sensuous and seductive, about the wealthy trappings of the newly-recovered prince. The *Pall Mall* reviewer's comment that the story is 'fleshly' is a fair one too, as though the story focuses on the sensuous appreciation of objects of production at the expense of a more thorough analysis of economics and politics of the situation of their making. But although there is a more sophisticated response to social questions in the story, we are not presented with the final results of the changes the young king will represent as if Wilde cannot imagine what the revolution will actually look like. The story retreats into the miraculous, even as it also states that the world must change: the 'how' of that change remains undetermined.

Indeed, it may well be the case that the story actually offers a swap: the politics of production for the sexual politics of desire, as McCormack's comments on the alternative meanings of 'fairy' stories imply. This is not such a big leap for a post-Freudian, post-Foucauldian and post-Bourdieu reader, for we know that rich and lovely objects may often stand in as displaced embodiments for desires that are forbidden, and we also know that the consumption of gorgeous objects is a trope of same-sex desire as it has been constructed and as it has constructed itself in the twentieth century and beyond. This may not be a message that 'innocent' readers will take away. Just like a poem such as Christina Rossetti's 'Goblin Market' (1861) where the luscious fruits sold by the goblin men are offered as elements of a seductive game, the innocent reader can choose to hear only the sensuous sounds of a temptation that is not precisely specified. 'The Young King' operates in a similar way, using lists of gorgeousness to seduce the reader with their display, while also offering a lesson in morality (or in political economy). We are told that:

> All rare and costly materials had certainly a great fascination for him, and in his eagerness to procure them he had sent away many merchants, some to traffic for amber with the rough fisher-folk of the north seas, some to Egypt to look for that curious green turquoise which is found only in the tombs of kings, and is said to possess magical properties, some to Persia for silken carpets and painted pottery, and others to India to buy gauze and stained ivory moonstones and bracelets of jade, sandal-wood and blue enamel and shawls of fine wool.

(CW: 214)

The objects are beautiful, but they are empty signifiers; they lead not to satisfaction of desire, but to its exhaustion, in part because the horrors of their manufacture, mining, or discovery, put into question: what is it one desires when the price of its ownership is misery or death? As we shall also see with *Dorian Gray*, they are also feminizing objects: jewellery, fine fabrics, and luxurious household goods from across the globe (and in some topical references, from the outposts of the British Empire and spheres of influence – India and the Middle East) belong more properly to the feminine sphere. There are, therefore, implied dangers in those goods beyond the dangers they pose to their makers: the danger of possession is a potential threat to proper masculinity. All of this implies that there are two distinct types of implied reader – a 'child' or childlike person (children like things – like to own and collect, as part of the process of defining who they are), and a more 'knowing' figure who will pick up another set of references to art objects that no child(like) reader could possibly understand.

When he first arrives at the Palace, overawed by the richness of his new surroundings, the Young King wallows in the unfamiliar experience of luxury, and by extension the reader is encouraged to enjoy the luxury too:

> Many curious stories were related about him at this period . . . On [one] occasion, he had been missed for several hours, and after a lengthened search had been discovered in a little chamber in one of the northern turrets of the palace gazing, as one in a trance, at a Greek gem carved with the figure of Adonis. He had been seen, so the tale ran, pressing his warm lips to the marble brow of an antique statue that had been discovered in the bed of the river on the occasion of the building of a stone bridge, and was inscribed with the name of the Bithynian slave of Hadrian. He had passed a whole night in noting the effect of the moonlight on a silver image of Endymion.
>
> (CW: 214)

Shades of Charmides are at work here. Wilde presents us with an image of a beautiful young man obsessed by beautiful artworks, and, as will later be the case with Cyril Graham, Basil Hallward and Dorian Gray, the art which fascinates him is focused on representations of young male beauty. Moreover, these are also fatal figures of male beauty, whose stories are tragic and whose desires are fatal. Adonis was the lover of the goddess Venus, and was killed while out boar-hunting; Endymion, in Greek mythology, was the setting sun, with whom the moon was in love, and who, as a result of this relationship, was condemned to everlasting youthful sleep – death by another name. The Bithynian slave of Hadrian was named Antinous, and is generally believed to have been the emperor's lover as well as his page. The young king also has an image of Narcissus in his chambers, the figure of a beautiful youth who fell in love with his own reflection, a figure who became a significant coded representation of the fatality of same-sex desire in the late nineteenth century. It is not just the love of any old art works. He is specifically interested in works of art that figure doomed male beauty, icons that speak (at least to some readers) of the homoerotic.

The young king is not, however, allowed to live merely in his sensuous aesthetic idyll. When he sleeps – in the classic formulation of the fairy story – he dreams three dreams that make him question his role as a king. His first dream takes him to a confrontation with the weavers who are making his coronation robe, one of whom tells him a few home truths about the relationships between rich and poor in capitalism, an important lesson in relation to the question of appearance and reality, because it shows his riches are always relative, and that one man's rich appearance is based on the reality of the poverty of others. The weaver tells him:

'in peace the rich make slaves of the poor. We must work to live, and they give us such mean wages that we die. We toil for them all day long, and they hoard up gold in their coffers, and our children fade away before their time, and the faces of those we love become hard and evil. We tread out the grapes and another drinks the wine. We sow the corn, and our own board is empty. We have chains though no eye beholds them; and we are slaves, though men call us free . . . The merchants grind us down and we must do their bidding. The priest rides by and tells his beads, and no man has care of us. Through our sunless lanes creeps Poverty with her hungry eyes, and Sin with his sodden face follows close behind her. Misery wakes us in the morning, and Shame sits with us at night. . . .' And he turned away scowling, and threw the shuttle across the loom, and the young King saw that it was threaded with a thread of gold.

(CW: 216)

This is clearly a more extended treatment of the small vignette of the seamstress in 'The Happy Prince', but it is also distinctly socialist in message: the poor are ground down by both material conditions (their poverty) and by ideology (the church requires them to accept their lot). They cannot see any alternative position. The Happy Prince sees misery, but not its larger, structural causes. The young king is forced to confront both the misery of the capitalist system, and his own implication in it: it is, of course, his own coronation robe that is being woven by the starving weavers.

With his second dream, the king again is shown how his wealth is amassed in the sacrifices of others. In this case it is a pearl diver who dies in order to bring to the surface the pearls for the king's coronation jewels: the details of the dream, with emphases on the naked bodies of slaves and slave drivers may also be significant, sexualizing the suffering they undergo, and suggesting very uncomfortable relationships between desire (for things, for people) and finance. The reader does not escape either, for we also consume both the things that are made and found for the king, seduced by their linguistic gorgeousness, and the men who gather them, described in similarly luscious detail, with the emphasis on an oriental cruelty in the slave-galley master, and the utter (but also attractive) vulnerability of the naked chained slaves (CW: 216). And his third dream takes him to ruby mines where he sees played out an allegory about greed and wealth through the figures of Death and Avarice. Again, he is also implicated in the human suffering, since the miners are toiling to produce rubies for his crown. The beautiful things that the king had ignorantly appreciated in his earlier phase are shown to have hidden costs. Beneath the surface of gorgeous appearance, there is a festering reality.

The young king seeks to change that reality through a new-found idealism rather than through politics; on his coronation day, he refuses the costly garments and jewels, dresses himself in the tunic of a goatherd and equips himself with a stick for a sceptre and leaves for a crown. The nobility think this is a joke when they see him; and the poor are also horrified by the revolution implied in his choice of clothing. A member of the crowd steps forward to remonstrate with the king:

> Sir, knowest thou not that out of the luxury of the rich cometh the life of the poor? By your pomp we are nurtured, and your vices give

us bread. To toil for a master is bitter, but to have no master to toil for is more bitter still. Thinkest thou that the ravens will feed us? *And what cure hast thou for these things?* Wilt thou say to the buyer, 'Thou shalt buy for so much,' and to the seller 'Thou shalt sell at this price'? I trow not. Therefore go back to thy Palace and put on thy purple and fine linen. What has thou to do with us and what we suffer?

(CW: 220, my emphasis)

While Wilde's narrative diagnoses the problems of the current system, he cannot work through to a solution: there is no 'cure' in the story. The young king, when the townsman speaks to him like this merely weeps, which speaks of 'sympathy' but which is hardly a practical response. The only solution comes from a supernatural source. Just as it looks as though the young king will be lynched by the mob, or the bishop will refuse to crown him, or some other disaster will befall him, God intervenes. The scene here in which the king is bathed in transfiguring light has biblical echoes as well as rather more profane echoes from the story of *Venus and Tannhäuser* as his goatsherd's staff flowers into a sceptre and the rest of his appearance is transfigured:[1]

He stood there in the raiment of a king, and the gates of the jewelled shrine flew open and from the crystal of the many-rayed monstrance shone a marvellous and mystical light. He stood there in a king's raiment, and the Glory of god filled the place, and the saints in their carven niches seemed to move. In the fair raiment of a king he stood before them, and the organ peeled out its music, and the trumpeters blew upon their trumpets, and the singing boys sang.

(CW: 222)

The repetitions of a passage like this speak back to the formulaic structures of the fairy story. Three times, in slightly different words, we see the description of a young man dressed like a king. Beyond the fairy-story elements, however, this image is also a profane mixture of the figure of Christ transfigured at the Ascension, and a pagan god, and it centres on the erotically attractive figure of a young man or boy, belying the assumptions of the genre.

The failure of the story in larger political terms is that it does not tell us what the king *does* during his reign. He may have the approval of God and the 'face of an angel' but it would also be good to know how he solves the conundrum of capitalistic slavery. There is a sense in which all that has happened is that the king has himself become one of the images that he worshipped in the earlier part of the story, a beautiful object without agency, made for the adoration of the people and a coterie audience outside the text. In that concentration on an idolatrous image, however, there is another type of politics: the politics relating to the veiled expression of a desire that makes young men its focus.

Wilde's fairy stories typically set out to show their audience what is wrong with the world, from individual perfidy to structural and social inequality, but they equally typically refuse to offer a solution to the problems they present, resisting the didacticism which is the raison d'être of the genre. At the end of 'The Devoted Friend', there is a tale within a tale, told to a selfish water rat; the linnet who tells the story comments ruefully to a passing duck:

> 'I am rather afraid I have annoyed him. . . . The fact is that I told him a story with a moral.'
> 'Ah! That is always a very dangerous thing to do,' said the Duck. And I quite agree with her.
>
> (CW: 293)

Wilde's narrator abdicates from the moral imperative that his original audiences viewed as narrative's primary purpose. Not having a moral, however, was also 'a very dangerous thing', as he was to discover.

Stories as Satire

With the four stories that make up *Lord Arthur Savile's Crime and Other Stories* (first published in volume form by Osgood McIlvaine in 1891) we come upon what we might really always have expected from Wilde – witty social satires that are rehearsals perhaps for the plays. This is Wilde being 'Wildean'. The four stories, 'Lord Arthur Savile's Crime', 'The Canterville Ghost', 'The Model Millionaire' and 'The Sphinx without a Secret' had all been previously published in different journals in 1887 before their collection and publication in book form in 1891. Unlike *The Happy Prince* collection they were not really intended to be read as a series. Nonetheless, they are connected in terms of their tone and their attitudes both to conventional society and to literary genre. Jerusha McCormack's remark that in the fairy stories Wilde was 'writing for himself' is less relevant here; in the more satirical short fiction, Wilde wrote deliberately for a knowing audience, focusing on what they thought they 'knew' in terms of genre, and upending their expectations. It is an argument that requires a little contextual background about the reading public of the period.

In the history of British publishing, the 1880s and 1890s saw a proliferation of new journals and periodicals of which the mainstays were the novel in serial form and the short story, often published alongside other non-fictional essays and discussions. Wilde was very well aware of this market, not least because he had worked as both a journalist and an editor. In Wilde's period, fiction was the material that sold magazines because the reading public could afford to buy relatively few books in volume form. This was a function of nineteenth-century publishing practices. Until the fall of the circulating libraries in the mid 1890s, books were artificially expensive, with a three-volume novel in hard-back format book costing around a guinea per volume: that is, a three-volume novel cost around a week's wages for the average working man and a substantial sum of money even for the middle classes. For volume-form publication, the circulating libraries in cahoots with the publishing houses operated a virtual cartel, inflating the cost of publication to ensure the market for borrowing fiction. Cheaper editions had begun to be published with the rise of the railway system and W. H. Smith's monopoly of book and news-selling at the stations (as Gwendolen puts it in *The Importance of Being Earnest*, one should 'always have something sensational to read in the train' (CW: 398)), but these editions tended to be 'late' publications of books where the limited borrowing and buying market had already been exhausted. Alongside those forms of volume publication, one with its relatively limited audiences (the circulating libraries prided themselves on the 'select' nature of both their commodities and their customers), one with a wider mass appeal, the tradition had arisen to make fiction available in serial form, either via in-house publisher's magazines, or (in the case of Charles Dickens) stand-alone serial forms. The serialization of popular fiction was particularly important for the magazine publishing industry, because the cliff-hanging stories kept the public buying: as Wilkie Collins had put it, writing of Dickens' phenomenal commercial success, the art of the novelist was to 'make 'em laugh, make 'em cry, make 'em wait!' The main fiction market was for novels, but short stories were popular too, often as fillers, so that a magazine would always be made up to the right number of pages – the reading public must always have value for money. And as fillers in the magazines, short stories would often take a rather sensational form. Particularly popular were detective stories and thrillers (Conan Doyle started publishing the Sherlock Holmes stories in the late 1880s in the *Strand* magazine, but tales of sensational crime had been appearing in magazines such as *Blackwood's* since at least the 1830s), ghost stories; and bodice rippers. These popular generic forms often exhibited purely formulaic features, as if there were a list of ingredients: a ghost story might, for instance, typically be set in a house that is not quite a home-from-home in that it is new to its inhabitants; servants and lower-class figures are generally more likely to be the subject of ghostly visitations; the tale is often narrated via a frame narrative, which is itself often set at the ghostly period of Christmas, and so on. It is conventions of this kind that Wilde sets out to undermine in the writing of his more satirical short stories, their repetitions and familiarity being precisely what his tales sought to resist. The disjunction of generic incongruity – comic versions of serious matters – is the source of their humour, and they would not have their effects if read by audiences for whom the genre had not been naturalized into formula.[2]

For Wilde's contemporaries, Arthur Conan Doyle had already established what a story entitled 'Lord Arthur Savile's Crime' should look like. The detective story required that the narrative focus on a crime committed by person or persons unknown; the great detective would bring his talents to bear on the matter, and, with some delays or setbacks, and perhaps an exciting chase through the fog-filled streets of London, he would unmask the criminal with a flourish, bringing him to book. For all the danger, excitement and horror of the criminal underworld, the real world would then be shown to be nonetheless a safe and explicable place in which the criminal is always caught, in which justice is always done, in which wrongs are righted through logical investigations and explanations, and in which the fruits of experience have logical and inescapable consequences. They are 'habitual stories', familiar and safe.

'Lord Arthur Savile's Crime' does not do any of these things. It begins, first of all, with a logical absurdity – the figure of Mr Podgers, the chiromantist, or palm-reader – who, we are asked to believe, really is able to read the future. Into the world of scientific investigation invoked by Wilde's title, comes a figure of the magical, of the inexplicable. Moreover the story hinges on the fact that Mr Podgers is not a fake, as one would generally expect in a detective story, where the detection of crime (and palm reading is often very close to crime) is the impetus of the narrative. The 'faith' of Wilde's narrative in Mr Podgers is unusual for the late nineteenth century where fakery was often expected in such contexts. For example, Robert Browning had written 'Mr Sludge, "The Medium"' as early as 1864, a poem which suggests that all such spiritualist concerns are a matter of mere confidence tricks. Even if Sherlock Holmes sometimes appeared to have an almost magical ability to read a person's character from external signs, he worked, according to the narrative's conventions, only on the best scientific principles, using the 'sciences' of phrenology and physiognomy in the context of ideas about degeneration to reach his conclusions. Moreover, there is humour in the man's very name: Podgers (like Sludge) does not inspire much awe as a name, suggesting a mismatch between appearance and reality, confirmed when the palm-reader is described by Lady Windermere to her guests:

> he's not a bit like a chiromantist. I mean he is not mysterious, or esoteric, or romantic-looking. He is a little stout man, with a funny, bald head, and great gold-rimmed spectacles; something between a family doctor and a country attorney. I'm really very sorry, but it's not my fault. People are so annoying. All my pianists look exactly like poets; and all my poets look exactly like pianists; and I remember last season asking a most dreadful conspirator to dinner . . . and do you know that when he came he looked just like a nice old clergyman, and cracked jokes all the evening?
>
> (CW: 161)

Given that Podgers' profession depends on the appearance of lines on a hand, the mismatch between appearance and reality – between signifier and signified – is comically significant.

Additionally, the trajectory of the story does not take the usual route. As Norbert Kohl argues, 'Basically "Lord Arthur Savile's Crime" is a parody on contemporary detective stories: instead of a search for the criminal, we have the character's search for the crime; his problem is to *become* a criminal, not to catch one' (Kohl 1989: 63). The parody is compounded by the story's subtitle, 'A Study of Duty', a very Victorian word whose earnestness is taken as a butt. The subtitle ought to imply that the direction of the text is towards a socially acceptable (conventional) sense of the word duty – a word whose usual meaning does not encompass murder (which is neither conventional nor acceptable). Two of the places in which the humour of the story arises are therefore the subversion of generic expectations in the narrative's structure and the subversion of socially acceptable forms of behaviour. It is a story that operates structurally through disjuncture.

These are not the only elements of humour in 'Lord Arthur Savile's Crime', which also contains what we might see as typically Wildean elements of social satire in its smaller details. The larger subversions are written into the smaller elements. For instance, Lord Arthur's reasoning for feeling that he 'must' commit the murder takes the conventional language of romantic love alongside the language of duty, and wilfully juxtaposes them both with murder, making murder the prerequisite for both love and duty:

> Ardently though he loved the girl, and the mere touch of her fingers, when they sat together, made each nerve of his body thrill with exquisite joy, he recognised none the less clearly where his duty lay, and was fully conscious of the fact that he had no right to marry until he had committed the murder.
>
> (CW: 169)

This is funny, but it is also a wickedly playful commentary on the automatic assumptions that underlie conventional behaviour. Like the creeds, which are effective because they are repeated, Wilde says, the behaviours that make social life possible are learned performances, not sincerely held beliefs. There is also much humour to be had from the way in which Lord Arthur sets out logically to work out who he should kill and how, in a reversal of the process of the traditional detective fiction in which the detective identifies victim, motive and manner *after* the event. In this case, Arthur makes a list of his relations to work out who would make the best victim, and is motivated in his choice not to pick someone from whose death he might profit (by being left something in a will) because the profit motive would lay him open to charges of vulgarity. Similarly with his choice of method:

> on arriving at the club, he went straight to the library, rang the bell, and ordered the waiter to bring him a lemon-and-soda, and a book on Toxicology. He had fully decided that poison was the best means to adopt in this troublesome business. Anything like personal violence was extremely distasteful to him, and besides, he was very anxious not to murder Lady Clementina in any way that might attract public attention, as he hated the idea of being lionised at Lady Windermere's, or seeing his name figuring in the paragraphs of vulgar society-newspapers. He had also to think of Sybil's father and mother, who were rather old-fashioned people, and might possibly object to the marriage if there was anything like a scandal, though he felt certain that if he told them the facts of the case they would be the very first to appreciate the motives that had actuated him. He had every reason, then, to decide on poison. It was safe, sure, and quiet, and did away with any necessity for painful scenes, to which, like most Englishmen, he had a rooted objection.
>
> (CW: 171)

There are shades of 'Pen, Pencil and Poison' here, but it is funny because of the mismatch between conventional behaviour and the utter immorality that it masks. Lord Arthur clearly has no moral sense at all. For him, the greatest crime is vulgarity – publicity in the newspapers, causing a scene, becoming a celebrity, upsetting the social expectations of his future parents-in-law are all more important considerations than the fact that he is about to kill someone. His morality is aligned purely to appearance. This social commentary rebounds in part upon the reader because we are placed in the text so as to share Arthur's point of view, at least briefly, and are supposed to buy into his reasoning.

A final example is the anarchist's bomb clock. Both for contemporary nineteenth-century readers and for modern readers today, bombs are really not a laughing matter. They were also a topical issue for Wilde's first audiences. There had been attempted anarchist outrages in London in the 1880s as well as Fenian attacks on public buildings. (Conrad's *The Secret Agent* (1907) and James's *The Princess Cassamassima* (1886) are both texts which deal with the atmosphere of anarchism and terrorism in late-nineteenth-century Britain.) In this case, however, the bomb, 'an ormolu figure of Liberty trampling on the hydra of Despotism', like the Remarkable Rocket, is a damp squib. (In general, the terrorist attacks in London had also been pretty inefficient, though their intent had been deadly.) In the words of the dean's daughter, the bomb fails to go off as intended:

> papa put it on the mantelpiece in the library, and we were all sitting there on Friday morning, when just as the clock struck twelve, we heard a whirring noise, a little puff of smoke came from the pedestal of the figure, and the goddess of Liberty fell off and broke her nose on fender. . . . When we examined it, we found it was a sort of alarm clock, and that if you set it to a particular hour, and put some gunpowder and a cap under a little hammer, it went off whenever you wanted. Papa said it must not remain in the library as it made a noise, so Reggie carried it away to the schoolroom and does nothing but have small explosions all day long. . . . I suppose they are quite fashionable in London. Papa says they should do a great deal of good, as they show that Liberty can't last but must fall down. Papa says Liberty was invented at the time of the French Revolution. How awful it seems!
>
> (CW: 179)

There are layers of irony here: that the anarchist clock that is supposed to bring liberty in fact destroys it; that the dean is clearly a very good potential victim for the anarchists, given his views on liberty but he remains unscathed; that an allegedly dangerous bomb is merely a child's toy; that for the dean's daughter, the most important question about it is whether or not it is fashionable.

Similar arguments about generic expectation can also be made about 'The Canterville Ghost'. The general function of the ghost story as genre is to leave the reader in that oxymoronic state of pleasurable terror. It achieves this function through the juxtaposition of unresolved supernatural elements with the real world, and the formulae are resolutely not comic. A 'proper' ghost story leaves elements unresolved and unsusceptible to naturalistic explanation at the end. The source of the thrill comes from a precisely opposite motion from that of the detective fiction: where the detective story is closed by the discovery and arrest of the criminal, the ghost story resists closure, and should leave the reader with a sense of continued mystery. Since what we don't know is what frightens us and since a literary text is a safe place in which to be frightened, the pleasure of terror is produced.

In 'The Canterville Ghost', however, only the ghost himself plays by the generic rules. Comedy arises from a situation in which it is the spirit world that is disrupted by the incursion of an utterly materialist and realist version of the real. The ghost himself is a collection of the stereotypical forms of ghostliness that are utterly familiar to all readers from whatever else we have read in the ghost story genre. In other words, the ghost's repertoire comes straight out of fiction – his reality, like Mr Podgers' powers, is undoubted, but he depends on the category of the literary for what he himself describes as the 'performance' of his ghostly role, acting out the part for 'hauntees' who do not know the rules.

> He thought of the Dowager Duchess whom he had frightened into a fit as she stood before the glass in her lace and diamonds; of the four housemaids, who had gone off into hysterics when he merely grinned at them through the curtains of one of the spare bedrooms. . . . He remembered the terrible night when the wicked Lord Canterville was found choking in his dressing room, with the knave of diamonds halfway down his throat, and confessed just before he died, that he had cheated Charles James Fox out of £50,000 at Crockford's by means of that very card, and swore that the ghost had made him swallow it. All his great achievements came back to him again, from the butler who had shot himself in his pantry because he had seen a green hand tapping at the window-pane, to the beautiful Lady Stutfield, who was always obliged to wear a black velvet band round her throat to hide the mark of five fingers burnt upon her skin, and who drowned herself at last in the carp pond at the end of the King's Walk. *With the enthusiastic egotism of the true artist, he went over his most celebrated performances.*
>
> (CW: 188, my emphasis)

In the performance of ghostliness, the effects depend, not on the spectacular nature of the acting, but on the credulity of the audience. As soon as he is pitted against those whose view of the world is purely materialist, he is defeated. The Americans wipe up his bloodstain with Pinkerton's Champion Stain Remover and Paragon Detergent (and how camply Washington Otis provides these solutions); when confronted with a ghostly figure with red eyes and clanking chains, they suggest merely that the chains need oiling; the Otis boys make their own ghost in effigy, and frighten the real ghost much more than he is able to frighten them, and so on.

The effect on the ghost of being treated with what he sees as 'gross materialism' is that he is forced, in turn, to see himself materially. This spirit has a real body, susceptible to bruising, and to being wounded by pea-shooters. The contorted logic of the original ghost story mode (where the spiritual mounts frightening attacks on the 'real' world) has been further contorted by the incursion of the real into the spirit world. Beyond genre, the point of the story is to comment satirically on the distinctions between the English aristocracy and American meritocracy. It is extremely important for the humour of the story that the ghost is most effective around English people who have been steeped in the traditions of their collective past, and who have a vested interest in believing in them. The Americans, on the other hand, are not nearly so easy to fool. Mr Otis comments at the outset: 'there is no such thing, sir, as a ghost, and I guess the laws of nature are not going to be suspended for the British aristocracy' (CW: 184). Even though he is forced to reconsider the existence of ghosts in the light of subsequent experience, he treats the apparition as a natural rather than a *super*natural phenomenon. Hence, there is no effect on him or his family from the incessant hauntings. In Wilde's narrative, this attitude is put down to the fact that Americans have no traditions; and without ever saying so in so many words, he is able to hold up both the English ruling classes with slavish adherence to tradition and American democrats who have no proper attitude to history to ridicule – a very satisfying position for an Irish author to adopt.

The last two stories contained in the collection are much slighter and shorter, and the satire and humour is rather less pointed. 'The Sphinx without a Secret' could be read as a satire on the contemporary woman of the 1880s and 1890s, the so-called New Woman. Taking the misogynist adage that one can never understand a woman's mind as its starting point, Wilde again weaves his story around the disjunction between appearance and reality, in this case an appearance of (possibly salacious) mysteriousness, which is not fulfilled. The narrator, looking at the photograph of the woman with whom his friend Gerald is apparently in love, comments:

It seemed to me the face of someone who had a secret, but whether that secret was good or evil, I could not say. Its beauty was a beauty moulded out of many mysteries – the beauty, in fact, which is psychological, not plastic – and the faint smile that just played across the lips was far too subtle to be really sweet. . . . 'She is the Gioconda in sables.'

(CW: 205–6)

That commentary on the woman's face is a very direct allusion to the description by Walter Pater of Leonardo's Mona Lisa:

She is older than the rocks among which she sits; like the vampire, she has been dead many times, and learned the secrets of the grave; and has been a diver in deep seas, and keeps their fallen day about her; and trafficked for strange webs with Eastern merchants . . . Certainly the Lady Lisa might stand as the embodiment of the old fancy, the symbol of the modern idea.

(Pater 1980: 99)

Pater's argument about the Mona Lisa is that she represents an ideal form of femininity through the ages, and that the key element of her desirability is her mysteriousness, the fact that she cannot be pinned down; that there is, in some way, a mismatch between her appearance and what she represents, not least because she is also an androgynous figure, and as Pater also argues, her face was used by Leonardo as his model for the male figures of Bacchus and St. John the Baptist too – yet another disjunction between easily legible appearances and the reality they represent. Thus, when the narrator tells Gerald that Lady Alroy is a sphinx without a secret, the answer does not close the mystery for Gerald, who continues to stare at the photograph of the woman who has fascinated him. Desirability is figured as that which cannot be exhausted by exposure or disrupted by explanation. It is though, a slight story, written probably precisely in order to reach the punch-line, that this woman, and by extension all women, are merely masks – apparently mysterious but actually empty.

'The Model Millionaire' is a different kind of satire based almost entirely on an extended pun, a feature that would be repeated in Wilde's work, particularly in *The Importance of Being Earnest*, where the name Ernest is a running joke. From 'The Model Millionaire's' title one might almost imagine oneself back in the world of the Wilde's fairy stories with their noun–adjective titles ('The Remarkable Rocket', 'The Devoted Friend', 'The Happy Prince', 'The Young King' and so on). Here the joke is on the word model, meaning artist's model for copying into art-forms, and role-model for copying into life's forms in a joke iteration of one of Wilde's most important themes, the relationship between life and art. The events of the story are very slight, and like the sphinx tale, it exists primarily to enable Wilde to indulge in a steady flow of witticisms about the nature of poverty, romance and art. Any attempt to read it seriously as a morality tale – a do-as-you-would-be-done-by story – would tend to make it rather more weighty than it is. It has the flavour of anecdote (possibly because it is allegedly based on a true story about one of the Rothschild family). And it subverts generic expectation precisely because it has no message and resists interpretation.

With the *Lord Arthur Savile* collection, Wilde moved into the literary milieu for which he was to become famous. From the fantasy never-never land of fairy-tales, he moved to contemporary London. The stories do not have overtly political messages; the fairy stories may be Irish in form, but they are not necessarily 'Celtic' or nationalist in tone. They do occasionally show homoerotic content, but the force of that content is muted, especially when we recall that the majority of Wilde's earliest readers did not necessarily seek it. It 'comes out' because late-twentieth-century readers are tempted to look for it. What these stories are, however, is intensely literary. They depend on a highly literate audience with well-defined generic expectations, which are then overturned. They may be slight, but they are not unsophisticated.

Chapter Four
Prose: Long Fictional

Picture Books

Where precisely in this book 'The Portrait of Mr W. H.' (first published in *Blackwood's Magazine* in July 1889) belongs is a very moot point. Others would certainly have placed it in a chapter on Wilde's critical prose, a perfectly reasonable location for it, since the majority of the story is made up of the ingenious theory of Shakespeare's muse for the sonnets, a theory that is derived from extensive historical and critical research. It is the kind of argument that belongs in criticism. Wilde himself was not sure how to classify it, but he seems also to have leaned towards the view of it as a critical work, in that he proposed it as an alternative chapter of the French edition of *Intentions*, to replace 'The Truth of Masks' (CL: 487). It certainly shares some of the 'playfulness' with critical convention that the other essays in that volume contain, particularly its bringing together of fiction and criticism into a single textual performance, which leaves neither mode untouched by its playful juxtaposition with the other.

I have chosen to discuss it here alongside *The Picture of Dorian Gray* for a number of reasons. In the first place, both of these two texts were extremely significant as 'evidence', called by the prosecution, in Wilde's trials in the spring of 1895. For prosecuting counsel, Edward Carson, they were clear evidence of Wilde's guilt of the crimes of 'posing as a somdomite' (the poorly spelled basis of the first trial) and then of gross indecency (the charge at Wilde's two criminal trials), though in Wilde's own terms, Carson himself is guilty of the critical sin of too literal an identification of the writer with his text. Carson's reading of that evidence in bringing the two texts together is also suggestive. The shared tropes that both texts elaborate – the fascination with youth, with the sexual ambiguity of boyhood, with visual artistic objects that are charged with subject status and with homoerotic potential, alongside their shared theme of contamination by dangerous influences, are continuations of ideas and themes that Wilde had touched on repeatedly throughout his writing. However, in these two texts, by accident of historical circumstance in terms of the hysteria surrounding the trials, they come to mean more than perhaps they had in other, earlier texts and contexts. Some of this is *post facto* reading, deriving from our 'knowledge' of what and who Wilde was. On the other hand, Carson could not have made his case, and probably would not have chosen to try to do so on a literary basis had it not been clear to him that the 'evidence' of the texts stood for more than an 'artistic' point of view. The charge of gross indecency, in other words, could be read even as early as 1895, into the evidence of these fictional texts.

A final element in bringing them together relates to the kinds of pictures that the images of Dorian Gray and Willie Hews are. As we have seen repeatedly, Wilde was often at pains to attack the basis of realist art, but in both cases, the paintings on which he performs his acts of *ekphrasis* (the process of describing and narrativising a painting) are intensely realistic, and this is part of their fatal glamour. Both narratives point out the extent to which realism might just damage one's moral health, a neat reversal of the normal assumption of the period, in which realism (so long as it was limited and had not become naturalism) was a literary mode that led to moral attitudes and behaviours.

Forgery

> Words are wise men's counters, they do but reckon by them: but they are the money of fools that value them by the authority of an Aristotle, a Cicero, or a Thomas, or any doctor whatsoever.
>
> (Hobbes [1651] *Leviathan*, Chapter 1, Part 4)

Thomas Hobbes, writing in *Leviathan* in the middle of the seventeenth century, argued that words have no necessary relation to the reality they are supposed to describe. The wise man uses them simply as an indication of meaning (a counter, root word also of 'counterfeit'), not as a guarantee; only a fool takes them for real money or real meaning. It is a view that Wilde might also have held. Forgery is one of the places in which relationships between words and reality, and between objects and their meanings, is most unstable. Certain kinds of written document are supposed to act as a guarantee of reality, and often of identity; the signature, for instance, guarantees identity in financial transactions, and, when applied to an artwork, supports the evidence of artistic authenticity that may also have a financial component. Forgery opens up a fault line in our conventionally held views about words and the world, and about truthfulness, sincerity and authenticity.

In Wilde's picture stories, the commodity or thing (the painting) is also painfully entangled in another form of exchange or intercourse: that of sexuality. Ian Small has argued that the twentieth-century response to Wilde's writing can be divided into critical works that focus on Wilde's relationships with his Irish background and nationality/nationalism (what we might call the Irish Studies Wilde), his relationships with other men (the 'gay' Wilde) and with theories of consumption and consumerism (the 'commodity' Wilde – where Wilde is both a commodity in the sense that his work and image were/are sold, and where he was himself a consumer of particular types of object, book and pleasure) (Small 2000). As Richard A. Kaye suggests, however, queer theories of Wilde's meanings (that is, theories that focus less on his biographical 'gayness' than on his capacity to trouble the taxonomic categories, often binary oppositions, which are supposed to guarantee meaning as stable and secure), tend to bring together the objects of consumption as indices of the subjectivities (including the sexual identities of those subjectivities) that consume them (Kaye 2004). *Dorian Gray* and 'The Portrait of Mr W. H.' are centrally concerned with the ambiguities that arise from the confusion of subjectivities and objects. Like Wilde's assault on generic expectation, the fact that he takes forgery as a central motif in the first of his picture books is an assault on the linguistic systems (and the values they inscribe) by which we understand the world. This is a fiction in which the relationship between words and authenticity, and the possibility that all value systems are faked is signalled.

At the centre of 'The Portrait of Mr. W. H.' there is, of course, a portrait.

It was a full-length portrait of a young man in late sixteenth-century costume, standing by a table, with his right hand resting on an open book. He seemed about seventeen years of age, and was of quite extraordinary personal beauty, though evidently somewhat effeminate. Indeed, had it not been for the dress and the closely cropped hair, one would have said that the face with its dreamy wistful eyes and its delicate scarlet lips, was the face of a girl. The black velvet doublet with its fantastically gilded points, and the peacock blue background against which it showed up so pleasantly . . . were quite of Clouet's style.

(CW: 302–3)

There are many things one might comment on in that description, in particular the strange androgyny of the painting's subject/object: a young man who might be a young woman, thus calling into question what Freud regarded as the single most important mark of identity: sex. The image's ambiguity also makes it strangely attractive. As Germaine Greer has suggested, the boy is 'beautiful when his cheeks are still smooth, his body hairless, his head full-maned, his eyes clear, his manner shy and his belly flat', but his attractiveness and beauty are extremely fleeting, which is partially the source of the fascination they provoke (Greer 2003: 7). And, because of the subject matter of the story, it is important to recognize in this figure of idealized male beauty one of Wilde's habitual tropes of homoerotic potential: the boy or youth. Since the theory that the story proposes is that Shakespeare's sonnets were largely written to a young man, not a young woman, that homoerotic image is certainly significant, not least because for some readers it would have been understood as an assault on national pride in the form of an insult to the manliness of the national poet. But there are other things to say about it too.

This is a word painting. The picture is not 'real' (even if it is realist) but is constructed in language. We can picture it, but we cannot hold on to it; it is a representation of a representation, not a representation of a real object. This is not Willie Hews, and it is not even a picture of Willie Hews, since, as the story repeatedly asserts, 'assuming the existence of the very person whose existence is the thing to be proved' (CW: 312) does not prove the existence of that person. The story dramatizes the deferral of the real, rather than its secure possession, and possessing the portrait risks being possessed (haunted) by it. Moreover, it can only be understood by reference to the artistic intertexts to which it alludes, implicitly the miniatures of Nicholas Hilliard and explicitly the paintings of Jean Clouet, thus making its relationship with the real even more attenuated. Additionally, a portrait is supposed to operate as some kind of guarantee of authentic identity in its resemblance to a real person. Portraits are very heavily invested with notions of authenticity and value; the sovereign's face on a coin or banknote is a guarantee of its value; portraits can even be used as a form of evidence in historical inquiry. The existence of the portrait of Willie Hews threatens the ideal of the authentic because the picture is a forgery that Cyril Graham has had made for him in order to shore up his theory about the origin of Shakespeare's sonnets. It acts as a false guarantee of a reality that never existed.

The significance of this event of forgery, therefore, is that it has the effect of falsifying a reality whose only existence is in language. In the story, the seriousness of the act of forgery, and the acts of interpretation that are founded on it, is that the faked evidence has 'real' effects in the real world of the fiction. Cyril Graham and Erskine both may be said to die for it. The story opens with un-named narrator discussing the concept of forgery as if it is a permissible artistic act, an argument Wilde had rehearsed more light-heartedly in 'Pen, Pencil and Poison':

> we had had a long discussion about Macpherson, Ireland, and Chatterton, and that with regard to this last, I insisted that his so-called forgeries were merely the result of an artistic desire for perfect representation; that we had no right to quarrel with an artist for the conditions under which he chooses to present his work; and that all Art being to a certain degree a mode of acting, an attempt to realize one's own personality on some imaginative plane out of reach of the trammelling accidents and limitations of real life, to censure an artist for a forgery was to confuse an ethical with an aesthetical problem.
>
> (CW: 303)

The discussion of Macpherson, Chatterton and Ireland signals an interest in the history of literary forgeries. James Macpherson (1736–96) had forged an ancient Irish myth cycle about Ossian, which had enjoyed enormous popularity across Europe in the eighteenth century. Thomas Chatterton (1752–70), at the age of seventeen, had been discovered to be the forger of a series of 'Medieval' lyrics. William Henry Ireland (1775–1835), most pertinently in this context, was the forger of a series of Shakespearean documents, including plays and poems. The narrator's first critical position is that forgery is simply an art form by other means, and confuses ethical (moral) with aesthetic considerations, and it typifies the very debates that had raged around the original forgeries, though in the course of the story that view will be modified.

The story's trajectory belies any certainty about the separation of ethics from aesthetics. The real intrudes on the aesthetic realm, crossing the boundary between life and art. In Chatterton's case (as his Victorian myth had it), the 'immorality' of forgery led to despair and suicide, which becomes, in turn, the fate of Cyril Graham in the story, and the fate that Erskine 'fakes', leaving his young friend to believe in his suicide, when in fact he dies of natural causes. Although Wilde's narrator asserts at the outset that moral law has nothing to do with the laws of art, he is forced to conclude, following Erskine's death, that just because a man dies for something does not make it true:

> [Erskine] thought that if I could be made to believe that he too had given his life for it, I would be deceived by the pathetic fallacy of martyrdom. Poor Erskine! I had grown wiser since I had seen him. Martyrdom was to me merely a tragic form of scepticism, an attempt to realize by fire what one had failed to do by faith. No man dies for what he knows to be true. Men die for what they want to be true, and what some terror in their hearts tells them is not true.
>
> (CW: 349)

In Christianity, martyrdom is supposed to be the supreme expression of faith. The unquestioning acceptance of godliness alongside the *author*ity of the writer is called into question by the story. The narrator ends his story in a peculiarly inconclusive statement. When friends admire the portrait of Willie Hughes, he does not tell them that the portrait is a fake. He merely muses to himself that 'I think there is really a great deal to be said for the Willie Hughes theory of Shakespeare's Sonnets' (CW: 350), even though the story itself appears to say that the theory is quite exploded by the act of forgery. It is as if the evidence evinced by the acknowledged forgery still has some claim to authenticity – for, if the fake has real effects, it may indeed be more potent than a genuine artefact. The story's oscillation between faith and doubt is dramatized in that final statement which negates any firm conclusion.

This celebration of forgery is at the heart of what came to be perceived as Wilde's attack on the values of Victorian masculinity. A man's self was defined by a series of coded signals – his dress and demeanour, his professional status, his marital status, and so on. These are what we might call external markers, which are supposed to signify the inner core of the proper man. In all areas of his life, the Victorian man was supposed to display his conformity to the ideal of the gentleman; and above all, he was supposed to be sincere – so that these outward markers of his conformity were to be read as an index of his inner nature. The problem with this, of course, as we've already seen with Wilde, is that it is very easy to counterfeit these markers, to pretend to be a gentleman, to forge an identity by wearing the right clothes, doing the right job, being married to the right woman: to play the part without inhabiting it. Wilde was a master impersonator, and impersonation is related to forgery – or fraud. In the course of the story, Wilde's narrator plays the role of the gentleman scholar. He reads Shakespeare's sonnets in a very careful way, and makes some extremely telling statements along the way about the relationships between truth and falsehood. Perhaps even more importantly, he implicitly connects the issue of forgery with the issue of homoeroticism and which are both behaviours criminalized by Victorian society, which, in their different ways, threaten the status of both the Victorian scholar, and the Victorian gentleman.

Shakespeare's name, in theory, acts as a guarantee of the potency of English literature. He defines Englishness. A working knowledge of Shakespeare was one of the guarantees of a Victorian English gentleman's status as an English gentleman since, along with his knowledge of the Ancient Classics it was the marker of his public-school and university education. The commentary on the sonnets provided by the narrator, with its excursions into the world of the homoerotic, is therefore quite a profound attack on the ideal of the gentleman as being above all heterosexual. Traditionally, the sonnets have been seen as a lesser part of Shakespeare's oeuvre. But in this story, Wilde's argument is that the sonnets are a kind of record of how the plays came to be produced; the inspiration for the plays came from the boy actor to whom the sonnets are addressed. The narrator comments:

There was, however, more in his friendship than the mere delight
of the dramatist in one who helps him to achieve his end. This was
indeed a *subtle element of pleasure*, if not of *passion*, and a noble basis of
for an *artistic comradeship*. But it was not all that the Sonnets revealed
to us. There was something beyond. *There was the soul as well as the
language of neo-Platonism.*

(CW: 324, my emphasis)

The emphasized phrases, 'subtle element of pleasure', 'passion' and
'artistic comradeship' all have the capacity to be read, particularly
this context and with the effects of their juxtaposition, as coded
references to same-sex desires. The narrator compounds this possible interpretation by going on to speculate that the sonnets show
evidence that Shakespeare had been exposed to translations from the
Greek of Plato's *Symposium*. The *Symposium* is a narrative account of
a dinner party, attended by Socrates and some of his followers (all
male), narrated by Plato, and of the conversation that took place
over dinner during which Socrates argues that love between men is
alone capable of satisfying man's highest ideals; the love between men
and women is to be regarded as inferior, a purely physical impulse
whose sole object is procreation, whereas the love of men for men,
while it may have its physical expression, is primarily noble and
cerebral. Wilde's narrative provides a list of the academic arguments
that suggest that some of the greatest figures of Western culture have
been neo-Platonists – that is, men who took male relationships as
their ideal. In particular, he mentions Michelangelo, Winckelmann,
Pico della Mirandola (in a homage to Pater, since all of these artists
were central to Pater's *Studies in the History of the Renaissance*), and he
thus places Shakespeare in a long tradition of the veiled expression of
same-sex desire.

Far from validating a conventional version of heterosexual masculinity, Shakespeare, in Wilde's version of him, dramatizes its
inauthenticity. Gender indeterminacy as played out on Shakespeare's
stage where there were no female performers belies the possibility
of making Shakespeare the representative of a normative masculine
heterosexuality. On these grounds, it is not in the least accidental that
this story, 'The Portrait of Mr. W. H.' appeared as evidence against
Wilde at his trials. The prosecutor Edward Carson asked Wilde:

Have you ever adored a young man madly? – No, not madly; I prefer love – that is a higher form. . . . I have never given admiration to anyone except myself. [Loud laughter] . . .

Then you have never had that feeling? – No. The whole idea was borrowed from Shakespeare, I regret to say – yes, from Shakespeare's Sonnets.

I believe you have written an article to show that Shakespeare's sonnets were suggestive of unnatural vice? – On the contrary, I have written an article to show that they are not. I objected to such a perversion being put on Shakespeare.

(Hyde 1948: 129–30)

The implied threat to Shakespeare, provided by a story that propounds a literary theory based on a faked portrait, rebounds into the real in an implied threat to the ideal English writer. His ideal English readers, the English gentlemen, were outraged by the implicit slur on their own authenticity, and indeed tendencies.

The Multiple Meanings of Dorian Gray: *Reading Perversity*

In the wake of the Wilde trials, as Ed Cohen has argued in *Talk on the Wilde Side*, the body of the text and the body of the writer were collapsed into each other, and the corruption of one was increasingly read as an index for the corruption of the other. *Dorian Gray* was certainly the text that did Wilde most damage at the trials. At the Queensberry libel trial, Edward Carson, acting in Queensberry's defence, returned over and over again to *Dorian Gray*, and the novel also featured strongly at Wilde's two subsequent criminal indictments. Carson made much of the fact that the novel had been revised between its publication in *Lippincott's Magazine* in July 1890, and its appearance in volume form in 1891. He sought to show that the revisions Wilde had made toned down what he construed as the book's 'objectionable content', and he referred to the volume edition as the 'purged edition'. The passages on which he concentrated in his attack on Wilde were all speeches by Basil Hallward, the artist who creates the portrait of the title. Hallward's declarations of love and fascination for Dorian were particularly pounced on, with Carson reiterating through his questions that the sentiments expressed by Hallward were (a) unnatural and perverse in themselves; and (b) could easily be read as evidence of unnaturalness and perversity on the part of their author. In particular he quoted two passages from the *Lippincott's* edition, both charting Basil's fascination with Dorian, the first in conversation with Lord Henry, the second in conversation with Dorian himself:

> When our eyes met, I felt I was growing pale. A curious instinct of terror came over me. I knew that I had come face to face with someone whose mere personality was so fascinating that, if I allowed it to do so, it would absorb my whole nature, my whole soul, my very art itself. . . . [Dorian] is all my art to me now. . . . You remember that landscape of mine, for which Agnew offered me such a huge price, but which I would not part with? It is one of the best things I have ever done. And why is it so? Because, while I was painting it, Dorian Gray sat beside me.

> It is quite true that I have worshipped you with far more romance of feeling than a man usually gives to a friend. Somehow I have never loved a woman. I suppose I never had time. . . . Well, from the moment I met you, your personality had the most extraordinary influence over me. I quite admit that I adored you madly, extravagantly, absurdly. I wanted to have you all to myself. . . . One day I determined to paint a wonderful portrait of you. It was to have been my masterpiece. It is my masterpiece. But, as I worked at it, every flake and film of colour seemed to me to reveal my secret. I grew afraid that the world would know of my idolatry.
>
> (Hyde 1962: 112–13)

To the reader who 'knows' what Wilde had done, these two passages seem particularly explicit statements of homoerotic attraction. Basil speaks of and to Dorian in the words conventionally associated with the male lover describing his relationship with a female mistress in heterosexual relationships, except, of course, that a heterosexual liaison would not (unless scandalously adulterous) need to be kept secret as Basil assumes that his idolatry for Dorian must be. On the other hand, nothing has actually been stated. It is up to the reader to infer whether the relationship described in these passages is immoral or illegal. The words make no mention of a sexual relationship; the precise nature of Basil's attraction for Dorian is not named. This lack of explicitness is reiterated in another passage that Carson read out in court, the passage in which Basil remonstrates with Dorian for his immoral life:

> Why is it, Dorian, that a man like the Duke of Berwick leaves the room of a club when you enter? Why is it that so many gentlemen in London will neither go to your house nor invite you to theirs? You used to be a friend of Lord Staveley. I met him at dinner last week. Your name happened to come up in conversation . . . Staveley curled his lip and said that you might have the most artistic tastes, but that you were a man whom no pure-minded girl should be allowed to know, and whom no chaste woman should sit in the same room with. . . . Why is your friendship so fatal to young men? There was that wretched boy in the guards who committed suicide. You were his great friend. There was Sir Henry Ashton, who had to leave England with a tarnished name. You and he were inseparable. What about Lord Kent's only son and his career? What about the young Duke of Perth? What sort of life has he got now? What gentleman would associate with him? Dorian, Dorian, your reputation is infamous.
>
> (CW: 112)

In April and May 1895, the suicide and voluntary exile of homosexual men was extremely topical, as an early review had noted in 1890. The anonymous review of the magazine edition (probably by Charles Whibley) in the *Scot's Observer* described *Dorian Gray* in terms that left no doubt about the sense that it was a corrupt novel by a corrupt writer, with the unspoken accusation being the crime of sodomy. The review stated:

> Why go grubbing in muck heaps? . . . Mr Oscar Wilde has again been writing stuff that would were better unwritten; and while *The Picture of Dorian Gray*, which he contributes to *Lippincott's*, is ingenious, interesting, full of cleverness, and plainly the work of a man of letters, it is false art . . . The story – which deals with matters only fitted for the Criminal Investigation Department or a hearing *in camera* – is discreditable alike to author and editor. Mr Wilde has brains, and art, and style; but if he can write for none but outlawed noblemen and perverted telegraph-boys, the sooner he takes to tailoring (or some

other decent trade) the better for his own reputation and the public morals.

(CH: 75)

This is a direct reference to an earlier and well-known homosexual affair. In 1889, following the so-called Cleveland Street Scandal, in which a number of upper-class and aristocratic men were suspected of making use of a homosexual brothel where telegraph messenger boys were 'laid' on as part of the entertainment, there had been a flurry of departures to the continent. Even more recently, and possibly one of the causes for Wilde being prosecuted at all, the elder son of Queensberry, Lord Drumlanrig, had committed suicide, it was rumoured, because his homosexual liaison with the prime minister, Lord Rosebery, was about to become public knowledge. The fatality of same-sex desire was a well-worked stereotype in the period, and suicide and exile were virtually stereotypical responses to disgrace on such charges.

Having read Basil's accusations aloud to the court, Carson asked Wilde if it did not suggest a charge of unnatural vice. Wilde's response was that it merely showed that Dorian Gray was a man of very corrupt influence. The precise nature of that influence was left unspoken. It could just be that Dorian is financially corrupt (that is certainly Dorian's defence, in part, when he comments that 'if Adrian Singleton writes his name across a friend's bill, am I his keeper?' (CW: 112)), and that he is a sexual rake among women. It could just be a charge of general immorality that is attached to his name, rather than a precise charge of unnatural vice.

Whibley's *Scot's Observer* review also offers a critique of the novel's moral and aesthetic qualities – indeed connects the two things. He describes the book as being 'false to art' because its subject matter belongs more to the discourses of law and medicine; as false to human nature, because Dorian is a devil rather than a human character; and false to morality, because the position the novel adopts in relation to Dorian does not make it clear that conventional morality is supported by the text. In other words, the novel offends against the conventions of late-nineteenth-century novel writing, and like many of Wilde's other works, it calls into question the very conventions by which the novel as genre can be understood.

It does this on a number of different levels, but most particularly in its refusal of the category of realism. The novel is predicated fundamentally on an idea of the impossible – that an art work can alter, by magic, or by some other supernatural agency, to reflect the state of Dorian's soul. On the one hand, the moral of the tale – that sin will out – is absolutely in keeping with Victorian tradition and with the so-called 'science' of degeneration, the view that evolutionary progress could equally be a matter for evolutionary decline and that the physical nature of a given being was absolutely a moral indication of their behaviour. As Basil remarks to Dorian:

> Sin is a thing that writes itself across a man's face. It cannot be concealed. People talk sometimes of secret vices. There are no such things. If a wretched man has a vice, it shows itself in the lines of his mouth, the droop of his eyelids, the moulding of his hands even.
>
> (CW: 111)

This is a commonplace of Victorian ideas about physiology and physiognomy. On the other, it is, of course, not Dorian's own face upon which the evidence of his sinful life is written, but that of his portrayed self. Realism eschews magic and the supernatural, but the book makes a realist point about the relationship between cause and effect using a non-realist plot item.

More importantly, perhaps, the text reverses the properties of the realist novel in its construction of Dorian's character. As Norbert Kohl argues, the text reverses conventional propositions about the meaning of fictional character. The traditional novel focuses on 'the moral and psychological expansion of protagonists who begin in self-absorption and move, through the course of a tortuous ordeal of education, to more complete self-knowledge.' The process of education 'leads them to a greater self-awareness, and helps them to establish a new personal and social identity' (Kohl 1989: 161). *Dorian Gray* in many ways reverses that order in which the 'hero's personality develops from selfish egotism to compassionate maturity.' Dorian begins an immature young man, and becomes increasingly selfish and isolated, as opposed to increasingly socially motivated and mature. He turns inward rather than outward, more Narcissus than David Copperfield. His self-consciousness does not lead to development, but to arrest or stasis. His state of arrested development is bound up with contemporary definitions of the meaning of art. When he looks at the painting for the first time, after he has heard the first part of Henry Wotton's disquisition on the meaning of life, Dorian cries out loud and makes his devil's bargain, predicting that the painting will 'mock me some day – mock me horribly!', which, of course, it will, but not as he thinks at this moment.

> How sad it is! I shall grow old, and horrible, and dreadful. But this picture will remain always young. It will never be older than this particular day of June. . . . If it were only the other way. [. . .] How long will you like me? Till I have my first wrinkle, I suppose. I know now that when one loses one's good looks [. . .] one loses everything. [. . .] I am jealous of everything whose beauty does not die. I am jealous of the portrait you have painted of me. Why should it keep what I must lose? Every moment that passes takes something from me, and gives something to it. Oh, if it were only the other way! If the picture could change and I could be always what I am now!
>
> (CW: 33–4)

What Dorian pleads for is stasis or fixity rather than change or development. He asks to become a work of art, which is static, as opposed to a living being, which is always in movement. In this movement, the novel rejects the potency of real life as it is represented in realism for an alternative (aesthetically perfect but biologically sterile, even fatal) mode of being. The preference for art over life (art for art's sake), becomes, in this novel, not just a tenet of aestheticism, but also a move into decadence, in what R. K. R. Thornton has defined as 'the decadent dilemma' where the decadent is caught between his desire for worldly experience and his attraction 'towards the eternal, the ideal and the unworldly . . . the incompatibility of the two poles gives rise to the characteristic decadent notes of disillusion, frustration and lassitude' (Thornton 1979: 26). The attempt to realize the ideal – to make the ideal real – is doomed and the attempt is fatal because it is a failure to recognize that it demands that Dorian become an object rather than a subject. His self-consciousness about his own beauty has the paradoxical effect that it does not support his subjectivity but destroys it.

What brings about the tragedy is a version of Dorian's image placed in the contemporary world; it is because the painting is realist, even if the novel is not. Basil tells us that he has painted Dorian many times before the fatal portrait at the heart of the novel. As part of the confession of his fascination for Dorian in Chapter 9, he speaks of the other images he has made of Dorian:

> I had drawn you as Paris in dainty armour, and as Adonis with huntsman's cloak and polished boar-spear. Crowned with heavy lotus blossoms you had sat on the brow of Adrian's barge gazing across the green turbid Nile. You had leant over the still pool of some Greek woodland, and seen in the water's silent silver the marvel of your own face. And it had all been what art should be, unconscious, ideal and remote. One day, a fatal day . . . I determined to paint a wonderful portrait of you as you actually are, not in the costume of dead ages, but in your own dress and in your own time. Whether it was the realism of the method, or the mere wonder of your own personality, I cannot tell. But I know that as I worked at it, every flake and film of colour seemed to me to reveal my secret. I grew afraid that others would know of my idolatry.
>
> (CW: 89)

Those other images of Dorian speak very loudly to an audience 'in the know' about the nature of Basil's idolatry. Paris, Adonis, Antinous and Narcissus, as we saw in Chapter 3's discussion of 'The Young King' are all figures associated with the perfected male body of homoerotic desire. As such, they stand as a code for 'knowing' audience; but they were also a very well-known code in a period where classical education remained the mark of the gentleman because it was so central to the public school curriculum. The 'knowing' audience, in other words, is not merely a coterie group of covert men-loving-men, but potentially includes any English gentleman. Nonetheless, in the representation of male bodies placed in mythological and historical contexts – the safe space of long ago and far away – the images are not scandalous. Basil's idolatry for Dorian only becomes a problem at the moment when it is placed in the 'here and now' – with Dorian presented in his own dress and in his own time, using a *realism* of artistic method. It is that representation which opens Basil's eyes to the nature of his attraction. He calls it idolatry, suggesting that it is profane in some way: he does not call it love or sexual attraction. The sin itself, whatever it really is, is still not named in the text. It is clear, though, that the fatal effect comes from making the ideal figure real, from crossing the boundary between the binary oppositions of life and art. It is also a joint sin committed by both Dorian and Basil, though in slightly different ways, since both fall in love with the image that Basil has constructed. The text finally seems to imply that Basil is a healthier figure than Dorian because his love is at least turned outwards towards another person, whereas Dorian is a Narcissus, in love only with his own image. His picture is so much a scandal that eventually he hides it away in a locked room, as if it were a pornographic or obscene text – which, of course, in some senses, it is.

Now all of this is not to say that there were not many other examples in late Victorian literature of non-realist fictions. Indeed, Elaine Showalter in her book *Sexual Anarchy* has argued that a great deal of male literature (written by and for men) took place in the realm of romance rather than in the realm of realism. Looking at books by Andrew Lang, H. Rider Haggard, Robert Louis Stevenson and Rudyard Kipling, among others, she argues that there was a whole masculine genre that avoided the world of domestic realism, which was supposed to be the norm in writing at this time. What distinguishes the adventure stories of writers like Haggard or Stevenson from Wilde's *Dorian Gray* is precisely that these other romances, with their elements of magic and the supernatural, were adventure stories that took place beyond the domestic realm, set, for example, largely in far-flung corners of the empire. Showalter calls this genre 'male quest romance' and defines it as a form of fiction in which heroes escape the domestic world of Victorian fiction into the exotic worlds of alien cultures. Magic of various kinds does take place there, but it does not threaten the solid views of reality held by Victorian England. This is a world where men are 'real men', defined by their machismo: where being able to shoot from the hip will save your life; where white women and the world they represent are profoundly absent and often despised.

In contrast, *Dorian Gray* is almost all set in domestic interiors. All three of the main male characters have a profound interest in interior decoration; as Dorian comments to Basil, 'you don't imagine I let [my servant] arrange my rooms for me?' (CW: 87). Neither Dorian nor Lord Henry is engaged in productive work; and Basil is an artist, working from home, whose status as an economic individual is therefore compromised in comparison say, to an industrialist or banker. These are men who live in the feminized sphere of the home as opposed to the masculine space of economics or adventure. On the few occasions when we see Dorian outside, he is wandering around the parts of London where no respectable gentleman should be – especially in the hours of darkness. All three men pay an inordinate amount of attention to their appearance. We are presented, in other words, with a world that is an all-male or homosocial as Eve Sedgwick describes it (Henry is married, but you hardly notice; Dorian's affair with Sibyl is over very quickly) (Sedgwick 1985); but the gender markers of conventional masculinity are all absent. Placing this fantastic story in contemporary London among a group of men who may actually exist, represents a profound threat to the meaning of proper masculinity at that time and in that space. Their proximity makes them risky. Basil, Dorian and Henry do not even have to be guilty of anything at all to represent something vaguely shocking to the ideal of the Victorian gentleman.

When Wilde read Whibley's review of his book in the *Scot's Observer*, he wrote to the journal with the following reply.

> It was necessary, Sir, for the dramatic development of this story, to surround Dorian Gray with an atmosphere of moral corruption. Otherwise the story would have had no meaning and the plot no issue. To keep this atmosphere vague and indeterminate and wonderful was the aim of the artist who wrote the story. . . . Each man sees his own sin in Dorian Gray. What Dorian Gray's sins are, no one knows. He who finds them has brought them.
>
> (CL: 439)

The onus of interpretation is placed, that is, not with the text or the author, but with the reader, a view Wilde put again in more epigrammatic form in the Preface he prepared for the 1891 version:

> Those who find ugly meanings in beautiful things are corrupt without being charming. This is a fault. . . .
>
> The highest, as the lowest, form of criticism is a mode of autobiography. . . .
>
> It is the spectator, and not life, that art really mirrors. . . .
>
> All art is quite useless.
>
> (CW: 17)

In these sayings among many others in the Preface, Wilde signals his disapproval of the theory of the realist novel whose aim was to reflect reality for the purpose of the moral improvement of the reader. Morality is a matter for the individual, rather than for the artist or his art, or for society at large. What you see in any text is a reflection of your own personality. By this argument, Whibley, who sees the novel as a muck heap and a subject for criminal investigation, has only his own dirty mind to blame. Yet, Wilde's novel remains very heavily implicated in the very conventional morality it seeks to mock; parody requires familiarity. The text cannot get its effects without a context of convention and generic expectations. The question of genre also matters in *Dorian Gray*.

Dorian Gray: *Gothic Text*

As Fred Botting (1995) and Elaine Showalter (1991), among others, have noted, there was something of a Gothic revival in the late nineteenth century. *The Picture of Dorian Gray* is in part a Gothic text in which Wilde made extensive use of the conventions of Gothic mode; but there is also a sense in which his text breaks with those conventions – hence Wilde's work yet again reproduces the notion of genre subversion. I want to suggest that because genre and gender are related concepts, what Wilde does in rendering one area (genre) of definition unstable has radical effects on the other (gender), and by extension on sexuality (one of the performance indicators, one might say, of gender).

Dorian Gray was written and read first in a context where there were a variety of well-developed models of Gothic fiction. It appeared, as I suggest above, when male quest romance was a particularly popular form, with the stories of Rider Haggard and Rudyard Kipling setting up an acceptable brand of male-defined Gothic – what Patrick Brantlinger has termed, 'imperial Gothic'. In Brantlinger's terms, imperial Gothic combines:

> the seemingly scientific, progressive, often Darwinian ideology of imperialism with an antithetical interest in the occult. . . . Imperial Gothic expresses . . . anxieties about the ease with which civilization can revert to barbarism or savagery, and thus [expresses anxieties]

about the weakening of Britain's imperial hegemony.

(Brantlinger in Pykett 1996 185–6)

Implicit in Brantlinger's argument is a strong dialectic between various oppositions: realism and romance; civilization and savagery; proper manliness and its various opposites. The imperialist project suggested that British men had to be 'real' men in order, to not only to conquer alien territories, but also to do so for the right reasons – bringing the light of civilization to the poor benighted savage.

The period saw, perhaps for the first time in the history of the Gothic, a concentration on the male figure as both hero and victim. The Gothic novel, as it was bequeathed to the late Victorian period, was largely one in which cultural anxieties were played out mostly on female bodies and on feminine sensibility. Traditional eighteenth-century Gothic fiction was filled with fainting heroines who lost consciousness just as the unspeakable spectre approached with deadly or dishonourable intent. Its landscape was the landscape of the romantic sublime – windswept cliff tops, stormy weather and haunted ancient castles through which the wind whistled its atmospheric discordances. As Fred Botting puts it:

In Gothic fiction certain stock features provide the embodiments of cultural anxieties. Tortuous, fragmented narratives relating mysterious narratives, horrible images and life-threatening pursuits predominate in the eighteenth century. Spectres, monsters, demons, corpses, skeletons, evil aristocrats, monks and nuns, fainting heroines and bandits populate Gothic landscapes as suggestive figures of imagined and realistic threats. This list grew, in the nineteenth century, with addition of scientists, fathers, husbands, madmen, criminals and the monstrous double signifying duplicity and evil nature. Gothic landscapes are desolate, alienating and full of menace. In the eighteenth century they were wild and mountainous locations. Later the modern city combined the natural and architectural components of Gothic grandeur and wildness, its dark, labyrinthine streets suggesting the violence and menace of Gothic castle and forest.

(Botting 1995: 2)

Perhaps the most important distinction between the eighteenth-century and the late-nineteenth-century Gothic is that at the end of the last century, Gothic came home. Whereas writers like Horace Walpole or Ann Radcliffe had habitually set their stories in some 'other' place, for preference in Catholic countries with extreme landscapes, Victorian Gothic is very often set in the here and now. Even in imperial Gothic, where the actual adventure takes place in Africa or India, it often comes home to England to haunt the memories of the protagonists who are nothing if they are not English gentlemen.

The notion of coming home is not just a question of geography: it is also a question of gender. The nineteenth century saw Gothic conventions increasingly as happening literally at home – rendering the home *unheimlich*, Sigmund Freud's term for the 'uncanny', which he defined as focused on the ambiguity that attaches to domestic space, where one is at once in a family (familiar) space, but where one may also experience one's most profound senses of dislocation and fear (Freud 1990). The eighteenth-century Gothic heroine/victim was punished for being outside the domestic sphere, in the wild landscapes of sublime nature, and in castles that were definitively not middle-class homes. The nineteenth-century heroine/victim was increasingly placed or imprisoned *within* the home and was punished there; and the threat offered by Gothic conventions was one played out on female bodies and minds. The Gothic has therefore largely been seen as a feminine mode that threatens femininity, and only by extension or vague implication threatens masculinity. Its manifestations in mid-nineteenth-century literature – Charlotte Brontë's *Jane Eyre* and *Villette,* or the Sensation novels of the 1860s – books written largely by and for women, has compounded this sense of Gothic as a feminine mode, offering vicarious adventure to women within the domestic sphere.

What differentiates the mid-century from the late-century manifestations of Gothic is the extent to which fear is played out in terms of the meaning of masculinity. Even imperial Gothic, with its evocations of the manly man, shows a sense of self under extreme pressure in which it is precisely the values of proper masculinity that are being tested almost – but not quite – to breaking point. Rider Haggard's heroes, for instance, almost all survive with their sense of proper manliness intact. The threat, in fact, becomes more radical and dangerous in London. A novella like Robert Louis Stevenson's *The Strange Case of Dr Jekyll and Mr Hyde* (1886) dramatizes the contamination of masculinity. Dr Jekyll's strange experimentations with his alter ego destroy not just Dr Jekyll himself, but also the friends with whom he has contact; one literally dies of terror as a consequence of seeing the effects of the double-self played out in his friend's change from one state to the other. The effects of Gothic coming home within a male community in the city of London, that is, rebound throughout that male community and attack the core value of masculinity. Again, in Bram Stoker's 1897 novel *Dracula*, while Dracula overtly threatens the women of England, his attack, when he comes to Whitby and London, is also an explicit attack on the core values of the men who surround these women – their science, knowledge, religion, potency (sexual and physical) and their values. No wonder he leaves the men, as well as the women he drains of blood, feeling drained and impotent.

Wilde's threat to the values of masculinity is more profoundly disturbing to late-nineteenth-century views. If *Dr Jekyll and Mr Hyde* suggests that there is an absolute other within the self, then Stevenson is writing a critique of nineteenth-century individualism in which the individual is represented as in fact divided against himself. This is a frightening thought, but it's not quite as scary as saying, as Wilde does, that it's not the Other that one has to fear, but the self itself. Although Dorian is inspired in making his devil's bargain by the philosophies of Henry Wotton, he must also bear responsibility for his own choices. Wotton acts as a bad conscience, the Gothic villain who tempts the innocent ingénue, just as Basil acts as a good conscience in a latterday version of the psychomachea (the struggle for the soul of Everyman by the forces of good and evil). Dorian has an equal choice about which path to choose, with Basil offering a direct counterbalance to Lord Henry's arguments. The responsibility for his soul is finally his own and his failure is to take an ideal image of himself for his essential being – to concentrate on the surface rather than on the depths of being, and to mistake the representation of the ideal for the ideal itself. The fault lies then within the self and its relation to its image; it is not then a question of self and other so much as a question of self and representation of self.

In his use of the portrait, Wilde situates his text within classic Gothic conventions. He may have been inspired, for example, by Edgar Allen Poe's short story 'The Oval Portrait', in which a painter is described painting a remarkable portrait of his own ideal love object, his wife – a situation that bears direct comparison with Basil's idealization of Dorian: the portrait as an object is part of the furniture of the Gothic interior, and often does more than its object status suggests it should. In Poe's narrative, we see the painter fall in love with the image he has created, unconsciously turning into a kind of vampire, feeding on the image of perfection:

> the painter had grown wild with the ardour of his work, and turned his eyes from the canvas rarely, even to regard the countenance of his wife. And he *would* not see that the tints that he spread upon the canvas were drawn from the cheeks of her who sat beside him. And when many weeks had passed, and but little remained to do, save one brush upon the mouth, and one tint upon the eye, the spirit of the lady again flickered up as the flame within the socket of the lamp. And then the brush was given and the tint was placed; and, for one moment, the painter stood entranced before the work which he had wrought; but in the next, while he yet gazed, he grew tremulous and very pallid, and aghast, and crying with a loud voice, 'This is indeed *Life* itself!' turned suddenly to regard his beloved: – *She was dead!*
>
> (Poe 1967: 252–3)

The parallels with Wilde's story are clear, but there are also key differences. In Poe's story, the critique of idealization rebounds on the painter rather than on the painted object/subject, since it is his consciousness which is central, whereas with *Dorian Gray*, it is the painted subject who is the centre of the reader's attention. But Wilde may, nonetheless, have adopted the trope of the portrait from this source. What he does with the convention, however, is to make it into a critique of the notion of the composite male self. Where Poe uses the convention to enact symbolic violence against the feminine, Wilde alters it to call into question the concept of the coherence of masculine identity. The Gothic effects of the portrait threaten manhood.

Mirrors and portraits are very much part of the Gothic world, for they both enact the possibility of doubling within the self. As Rosemary Jackson has argued,

> the mirror [is] a frequent motif in literature, as a metaphor for the production of other selves. A mirror produces difference. It establishes a different space, where our notions of self undergo radical change. It is 'a spatial representation of an intuition that our being can never

be enclosed within any present formulation – any formulation here and now – of our being.' By presenting images of the self in another space (both familiar and unfamiliar), the mirror provides versions of self transformed into another, become something or someone else. It employs distance and difference to suggest the instability of the 'real' on this side of the looking-glass and it offers unpredictable (apparently impossible) metamorphoses of self into other.

(Jackson 1981: 87–8)

On the one hand, the mirror is a standard metaphor for the representation of the real – indeed, one of the key metaphors of Realism is that of 'holding a mirror up to nature'. On the other, the mirror is a framed space – like the space of a picture. It limits point of view and partially aestheticizes the real. Representing the self to the self, it shows up that there is difference in the same, a tension in the self that calls into question the idea of the individual as an undivided thing. A realistic portrait is very likely to have the same effects. Like the mirror, it represents the self to the self through the interpretation of another: the media of light and paint, the mediation of the painter and the mediation of the subject's position in relation to his representation. A mirror is a perfect portrait: and it should never lie, as the story of Snow White attests: the wicked stepmother's mirror, used to bolster up her image of herself as a sexually potent figure cannot lie when she is no longer 'the fairest of them all'. In the context of *Dorian Gray*, produced in a highly gendered culture, the mirror is also a feminine object, and the attention one pays to the external self is figured as something women do, and 'real' men don't. Dorian's relationship with his own image, therefore, although he is male, is a further instance of his feminization, along with his aristocratic, idle lifestyle, his interest in interior decoration, jewellery, perfume and clothing.

In Wilde's novel, however, it is the image in the mirror which lies, and the portrait which alters through time to tell the truth. Dorian comments that the portrait 'had taught him to love his own beauty' (CW: 75). But it is also the mirror image of his degradation: 'The quivering ardent sunlight showed him the lines of cruelty round the mouth as clearly as if he had been looking into a mirror after he had done some dreadful thing.' (CW: 74) And as time goes on, Dorian is so trapped in his image that he comes to loathe seeing the false perfection of a mirrored self in reflection almost as much as he dreads seeing the moral truth of the portrait itself: he dreads polished surfaces and still water, which would confirm by their images of him what he has become – ironically, the absence of signs of ageing and degradation become precisely the markers of his moral corruption. Almost the last thing that Dorian does before he stabs his portrait is to break a mirror:

> The curiously carved mirror that Lord Henry had given him, so many years ago now, was standing on the table, and the white-limbed Cupids laughed round it as of old. He took it up, as he had done on that night of horror, when he had first noted the change in the fatal picture, and with wild, tear-dimmed eyes looked into its polished shield. . . . he loathed his own beauty, and, flinging the mirror on the floor, crushed it into silver splinters beneath his heel. It was his beauty that had ruined him, his beauty and the youth that he had prayed for. But for those two things, his life might have been free from stain. His beauty had been to him but a mask, his youth but a mockery.
>
> (CW: 157)

Dorian's image is produced here as an aestheticized, idealized image, framed by an antique frame, just as if his reflection is also a work of art: the stasis of the mirror image is perversely the stasis of an artwork. Breaking the mirror, however, does not destroy the image, which still has two living embodiments – Dorian himself and the picture. And it is highly significant that Dorian seeks to release himself from the bondage of his bargain by a vandal attack on his painted image. The image has crossed the boundary between art and life, between representation and reality: the painted image *is* Dorian's self.

> [The picture] had been conscience. He would destroy it. He looked round and saw the knife that had stabbed Basil Hallward. . . . As it had killed the painter, so it would kill the painter's work and all that meant. It would kill the past, and when that was dead he would be free. It would kill this monstrous soul-life, and, without its hideous warnings he would be at peace. He seized the thing and stabbed the picture with it. There was a cry heard, and a crash. The cry was so hideous in its agony that the frightened servants awoke, and crept out of their rooms.

When would-be rescuers enter the locked room in which Dorian and his image are to be found:

> they found, hanging upon the wall, a splendid portrait of their master as they had last seen him, in all the wonder of his exquisite youth and beauty. Lying on the floor was a dead man, in evening dress, with a knife in his heart. He was withered, wrinkled, and loathsome of visage. It was not till they had examined the rings that they recognized who it was.
>
> (CW: 158–9)

Along with the notion of the double, the novel also draws on the developing Gothic conventions of the city as a space of unspeakable horrors and moral danger. One of the fundamental symptoms of Dorian's developing depravity is his use of city space, and in particular his journeys into parts of London which are 'forbidden territories'. As various critics and historians have argued, London was a place with clearly demarcated areas that registered the morality or otherwise of those who inhabited those streets or who passed through them. We see Dorian in the streets twice; once after he has deserted Sibyl, and once after the murder of Basil, and the trauma of the disposal of his body. In these two excursions, the city streets take on something of the atmosphere of traditional Gothic architecture and landscape. 'This also has been one of the dark places of the earth,' says Conrad's Marlow of London in *Heart of Darkness* (1900). London, that is, is a city of ambivalence. On the one hand it is the heart of a vast empire bringing enlightenment to the rest of the world. It contains the 'mother of parliaments', an enlightened judiciary, and the marks of English national identity, with statues of national heroes, national galleries, national commerce and other monuments to its national culture dotted through its environs. On the other hand, it is also the city through which Jack the Ripper had stalked in the winter of 1888–89, and the news of his gruesome murders in the poorest areas of Whitechapel in the East End had entered the middle-class respectable homes of west London through the sensational reporting of their newspapers. What Jack the Ripper's story did was to 'bring home' to the middle classes the proximity of problems of poverty, crime and violence to themselves. The line between West End and East End is not, after all, a secure marker of social and moral distinctions. As Judith R. Walkowitz argues in her book *City of Dreadful Delight*:

> The literary construct of the metropolis as a dark, powerful, and seductive labyrinth held a powerful sway over the social imagination of sophisticated readers. It remained the dominant representation of London in the 1880s, conveyed to many reading publics through high and low literary forms, from Charles Booth's surveys of London poverty to the fictional stories of Stevenson, Gissing and James, to the sensational newspaper exposés by W. T. Stead and G. R. Sims. These late-Victorian writers built on an earlier tradition of Victorian urban exploration, adding new perspectives of their own. Some rigidified the hierarchical divisions of London into a geographic separation, organized around the opposition of East and West. Others stressed the growing complexity and differentiation of the world of London, moving beyond the opposition of rich and poor . . . to investigate the many class cultures in between. Still others . . . repudiated a fixed, totalistic interpretative image altogether, and emphasized instead a fragmented, disunified, atomistic social universe that was not easily decipherable.
> (Walkowitz 1992: 17)

In the cold light of day, Dorian Gray belongs absolutely to the respectable middle classes who defined the meaning of Victorian culture. But at night, a different self emerges, encouraged by Lord Henry's advice to find as much experience as possible. The only respectable way for figures of Dorian's social class to enter the stews of east London was as a charity worker, and we hear of him, early in the novel, for example, being dragooned into volunteering to play duets on the piano for the poor by Lord Henry's Aunt Augusta. Charity work, on the other hand, was largely viewed as a pastime for respectable women (who could not work outside the home except as charity workers, for which there would be no economic reward, hence leaving their dependent status unthreatened). For Dorian to be involved – even though he actually doesn't go to the concert as promised – is a mode of feminization. Beyond charity work, the only reason for a respectable man to be found in the East End was for unrespectable (sexual or drug-related) motives. When Dorian himself explains to Lord Henry how he came across Sibyl Vane, for example, it is to those less than salubrious purposes that he alludes:

one evening, about seven o'clock, I determined to go out in search of some adventure. I felt that this grey, monstrous London of ours, with its myriads of people, its sordid sinners, and its splendid sins, as you once phrased it, must have something in store for me. . . . I don't know what I expected, but I went out and wandered eastward, soon losing my way in the labyrinth of grimy streets and black, grassless squares.

(CW: 47)

Dorian has gone to the East End in search of 'adventure', which he ought more properly to seek in the east of empire, India or Africa, whereas 'adventure' in the East End certainly had illicit connotations. His loss of his way in the labyrinth of city streets is both a literal description of being physically lost, and a metaphorical description which inscribes the beginnings of Dorian's loss of his true sense of self. The very figures of melodrama are to be found in the East End: there is the evil Jew who runs the theatre (like Fagin); the sentimental mother; the brother who is about to go to Australia in an attempt to make his fortune; and the beautiful girl whom Dorian hopes to rescue from her background – at least until she falls in love with him and ruins her artistry in the process. Melodrama and Gothic are related genres; and Dorian describes Sibyl as 'absurdly melodramatic' (CW: 73) when he ceases to love her. He then brings back the corrupted atmosphere of the East End back with him to his West End home. It is, of course, his cruelty to Sibyl and her suicide as a result of it that brings about the first change in the portrait in the form of a 'touch of cruelty about the mouth' (CW: 74). When he breaks away from her, he loses himself (again literally and metaphorically) in the city:

In a few minutes he was out of the theatre. Where he went to he hardly knew. He remembered wandering through dimly-lit streets, past gaunt black-shadowed archways and evil-looking houses. Women with harsh voices and harsh laughter called after him. Drunkards had reeled by cursing, and chattering to themselves like monstrous apes. He had seen grotesque children huddled upon doorsteps, and heard shrieks and oaths from gloomy courts.

(CW: 73)

The atmosphere of Gothic darkness, in which the familiar sights of poverty in the city are rendered as monstrous, alien and strange, only lifts when he reaches Covent Garden (in the west) towards dawn.

Similarly, in Chapter 16, after Dorian has arranged for the disposal of Basil's body, he seeks oblivion in the East End, in 'the sordid shame of the great city'. Dorian becomes a liminal figure, one who crosses boundaries between spaces. In moving from east to west and back again in London, he is constantly re-crossing invisible lines which signalled to Victorian Londoners the distinction between morality and respectability and their opposites. Moving into an unrespectable geography has implications about Dorian's place in the moral economy. He brings the contamination of the east back with him to the west; and he seeks to forget what he has done in the west in the stews of the east. Thus is Dorian's gender identification threatened on two counts: he is feminized by his reliance on external signs – his appearance, his clothes, the admiration of his friends; and his inner corruption threatens his status as a proper gentleman who would not, of course, do such things.

The force of Gothic texts in general is that they provide a space for the articulation of forbidden things, and they make cultural anxieties, displaced through fantastic plot elements, into the subject of their fictions. They speak the 'unspeakable', as Eve Sedgwick has argued, unspeakable being, she says, is a favourite Gothic word (Sedgwick 1980: 4). In the wake of the Wilde trials, unspeakable was one of many code words that articulated the possible presence of same-sex desire, as well as elements of the Gothic. In Sedgwick's *Between Men*, she suggests that there is a matrix of associations between the conventions of Gothic literature, the implications of decadence, and the presence of homosexuality.

> When I began to read Gothic novels . . . it was because they had an alluring reputation for decadence. Decadence is a notably shifty idea, but clearly its allure . . . lies in its promise of initiatory shortcuts to the secret truths of adulthood. The secrets of its sexuality are represented by its practices (most explicitly incest and rape) that run counter to the official version. In a close relation with these, the secrets of class are represented in decadent literature by elements of the bourgeoisie that can disassociate themselves from the productive modes of their class, and, by learning to articulate an outdated version of aristocratic

values, can seem to offer some critique of – some ready leverage on – the bourgeois official culture. . . . the Gothic was the first novelistic form in England to have close, relatively visible links to male homosexuality, and even its visibility and distinctness were markers of division and tension between classes as much as between genders.
(Sedgwick 1985: 90–1)

Sedgwick argues that the Gothic is a mode explicitly linked with the forbidden (and *Dorian Gray* was of course written at a time when nothing was more forbidden than same-sex desire). The subject matter of the Gothic is primarily sexual (even if the sexuality is often displaced), and it is also perverse – hence the mentions of incest and rape, which were essential elements in romantic Gothic novels by men. For instance Matthew Lewis's *The Monk*, and *Melmoth the Wanderer* by Wilde's great uncle, Charles Maturin, both deliberately focus on violent and quasi-pornographic forbidden sexual activities. The articulation of the forbidden offers, Sedgwick suggests, a threat to the society that does the forbidding – official bourgeois culture. There is also a class element to the Gothic, which comes up in *Dorian Gray* where the main characters are not economically productive as they should be as proper members of official bourgeois culture. Their attitudes proclaim them as aristocrats, who, among all the other sexually forbidden things they are rumoured to do by the middle classes, are presented as effeminate dandy figures – as prototypical gay men, in one set of possibilities, or as aggressively heterosexual rakes in another. In this view Dorian offends proper masculinity on every count: he is an effeminate-looking man, who is over-interested in his appearance; he has no economic role; he is geographically mobile to a much greater extent than any respectable gentleman should be; he acts out the role of aristocrat rather than bourgeois gentleman; and in all these ways, he contaminates the official version of the middle-class home by bringing elements of the Gothic into it. Sexual ambiguity, as I have argued elsewhere, is a major feature of Gothic effects. The combination of a series of border crossings makes Dorian a particularly risky figure.

Finally, then, Gothic conventions have a tendency to naturalize the perverse. In a text so explicitly set in contemporary London (we must remember that Dorian's portrait is a picture of him in modern dress, and painted with realistic technique) the perverse in all those spheres – from the sexual to the geographic – comes home. *Dorian Gray* domesticates and naturalizes the Gothic, which is much more threatening than a more 'way-out' story set somewhere else in some other time would be.

Chapter Five
Plays

Wilde wanted to be a playwright right from the start. This should come as no surprise. Given that one of his major concerns was with the relationship between life and art, where better to seek that relationship than on the stage, where, like a portrait, life is 'framed' by a proscenium arch, untouchable and often idealized, but where, unlike a portrait, the figures depicted are set into motion and action. The evidence of *The Picture of Dorian Gray* would also tend to suggest that Wilde liked the slightly seedy glamour of the theatre, and its reputation for raciness. The space where Sibyl Vane performs is a world both real and unreal, simultaneously fantastic and sordid. The architecture is a kitsch fantasy, 'like a third-rate wedding cake' says Dorian, and is peopled with a plebeian audience that engages in a 'terrible consumption of nuts' (CW: 48). The scenery and costumes are terrible, and the acting is feeble:

> Romeo was a stout elderly gentleman, with corked eyebrows, a husky tragedy voice, and a figure like a beer-barrel. Mercutio was almost as bad. He was played by the low-comedian, who introduced gags of his own and was on most friendly terms with the pit. They were both as grotesque as the scenery, and that looked as if it had come out of a country booth.
>
> (CW: 49)

Nonetheless, Sibyl can play a convincing Juliet even here, despite the failings of her Romeo and her context. Her performed sincerity is in disjunction with the tawdry make-believe of everything else. Yet despite all the disgust that Dorian expresses for this place, it is dangerously attractive, even addictive to him. Both Henry and Basil complain that they never see him anymore, and the reason is simply that he cannot keep away – 'I get hungry for [Sibyl's] presence,' he tells them (CW: 51). What he feels, of course, is desire. Sibyl's performances are calling him into being as a person in a play – in a love story if she were to write the script; in Wilde's script, it's a melodrama.

Sibyl's world, after all, is not one of 'respectable' theatre people: it is a world of melodrama, fictionality and overwrought gestures, which owes as much to Dickens's depictions of the theatre (in *Nicholas Nickleby*, and in *Great Expectations*) as it does to any observation of a real East End hall. Her faded mother with her exaggerated gestures and desperate need for an audience is just one symptom of the sordid, louche atmosphere. The atmosphere in this theatre is poisonous and infectious. Even James Vane, Sibyl's younger brother, who hates the theatre and all it stands for, cannot stop himself from falling into the melodramatic gesture and speech. As Sibyl says to him when he has uttered dark threats about Prince Charming's intentions: 'You are like one of the heroes of those silly melodramas that mother used to be so fond of acting in' (CW: 61). In this atmosphere, Dorian himself becomes first a fairytale figure, a player applauding the actress from the stalls, and thereafter participating in the performance himself, even if this is a Prince Charming without much of the charm who becomes the mustachio-twisting villain. In Dorian's world, all the world is indeed a stage. (The conversations of Dorian Gray with his upper-class acquaintance are certainly staged performances, straight out of the comedy of manners, and indeed occasionally repeated word for word by characters on the Wildean stage.) There is no significant action that has not been predicted by previously existing generic conventions – the sensation novel, the Gothic novel, Renaissance drama, melodrama. Lord Henry recognizes this, describing Dorian's affair with Sibyl as 'a rather commonplace *début*' (CW: 47) that any romance hero might fall into, and Sibyl's death as 'a strange lurid fragment from some Jacobean tragedy' (CW: 82). Life is merely a series of stylized gestures copied and called into being by fictional counterparts. The script is already written: we know already that lords and actresses don't often stand much of a chance of 'happily ever after' endings; more than that, we know that Sibyl's mother has already lived out the tragedy that probably awaits Sibyl if she and Dorian get it together – the abandoned mistress of two bastard children, a 'woman of no importance' as Wilde himself would later dramatize this figure. Thus it should be no surprise that Prince Charming quickly turns into a stage villain. When he turns on her for her lousy performance as Juliet, Sibyl pleads: 'You are not serious, Dorian? . . . You are acting' (CW: 72). And, of course, he is, and so is she:

> [Sibyl] crouched on the floor like a wounded thing, and Dorian Gray, with his beautiful eyes, looked down at her, and his chiselled lips curled in exquisite disdain. . . . Sibyl Vane seemed to be absurdly melodramatic. Her tears and sobs annoyed him.
>
> (CW: 73)

But just who is being melodramatic there? Wilde is able to have Dorian sneer at the conventions of the melodrama while getting full benefit out of them.

Unsurprisingly, perhaps, Wilde's first attempts at drama have pretty strong melodramatic elements. In the period of his trip to America in the early 1880s he had managed to sell his first early theatrical product to the American actress Marie Prescott. *Vera or the Nihilists* (privately printed in 1880 and with an acting edition printed in 1882) opened in New York in August 1883, following an aborted attempt to mount a production with Mrs Bernard Beere's company in London in 1881. The production, in the words of Katharine Worth, was 'not a success, closing after a week to notices which contained some praise, but were on the whole dismissive, even rudely so' (Worth 1983: 26). *Vera* is not a great play, though it has some interesting moments. It tells Vera's story as a conflict between her 'natural' desires as a woman to love and cherish her man (who just happens to be the Czarevich, and therefore her political enemy), and her political engagement with the nihilist movement in mid-century Russia. It is largely overwrought (as is its heroine) and melodramatic (in its plot), though it does contain some of the epigrammatic wit for which Wilde would later become famous in the 1890s, particularly coming in the lines of the dandiacal figure of Prince Paul, whose cynicism and distance from the suffering with which the rest of the play is concerned is couched in the 'perfectly phrased' sentences for which Wilde's later dandies would become renowned.

The archaeological interest attaching to this earliest of the plays, though, is not the focus of this chapter. It is the 1890s plays that made Wilde's reputation as a playwright and that should have made him rich, had not the disaster of 1895 befallen him. Wilde became successful in the theatre for two main reasons: firstly, as Josephine Guy and Ian Small amply demonstrate, he was fortunate in his relationships with intelligent actor-managers, particularly George Alexander who produced the first outings of *Lady Windermere's Fan* (February 1892, St James Theatre London) and *The Importance of Being Earnest* (February 1895, also at the St James). Secondly, in the well-made plays of the 1890s, including *Lady Windermere* and *Earnest*, *A Woman of No Importance* (April 1893) and *An Ideal Husband* (January 1895) Wilde found a genre to which he could make interesting modifications. Kerry Powell's brilliant book *Oscar Wilde and the Theatre of the 1890s* (1990) demonstrates the extent to which he was indebted to the theatre of his age, drawing plot elements and staging from the variety of drama that he had seen onstage, often in the role of critic during the 1880s and 1890s. Though this research more than suggests that the charge of plagiarism often levelled against Wilde was deserved (Powell enumerates multiple examples of Wilde's 'borrowings', adaptations and downright thefts from the works of his contemporaries), it is his insertion into the conventions of the period, and his adaptation of them that made him, in the words of one contemporary theatre critic, J. T. Grein, writing in an obituary notice in 1900, a playwright who could produce work that was 'different withal from every kind of play of native production' (CH: 235). In his well-made plays, Wilde used the generic conventions he had studied as a critic, but used them against the grain. The plays were successful, though it has to be said that they are slightly repetitive: in Grein's words, 'they all run more or less on the same lines. They are what one could call society plays, pictures of fashionable life in which an unmistakable air of reality is happily wedded to playful satire' (CH: 233). Genre forms, of course, are repetitive, which is how they get their effects. What Wilde does with genre here, as elsewhere, is play games with the repetitions. The society plays were commercial objects and as such, their subversions are limited though in the playing, particularly in the contemporary theatre from the 1990s onwards, subversion has been very successfully 'played into' them, as John Stokes's discussions of the 1990s' West End productions shows (see Stokes 1996). And this has tended to lead to a view of Wilde as steeped in a tradition that he did not make and which he does not control, a view that takes the comedies as conservative objects.

There is, however, another Wilde the playwright. In the two

sections of this chapter, I discuss the 'conservative' and commercial Wilde; and then the much experimental Wilde. In the first part of the chapter, the focus is on *Lady Windermere's Fan*. The later plays follow many of the same patterns that one finds in the first successful effort, and all are actually based on the same basic theme: that of the double standard of expectations in behaviour for men and women. Mrs Arbuthnot is *The Woman of No Importance*, a 'fallen woman' whose sexual past excludes her from social acceptance; the ideal husband falls similarly foul of the failure to live up to the ideals of his wife (which are not in fact at all dissimilar from Lady Windermere's ideals about her husband). Perhaps strangely, I want to suggest that *The Importance of Being Earnest* has some claim to being described as an avant-garde drama, and the second part of the chapter places *Earnest* in the same context as Wilde's most obviously experimental play, *Salomé* (published in French in 1891 and first performed in Paris in 1896).

Selling Out? Wilde, the Commercial Theatre and Lady Windermere's Fan

Wilde's first commercially successful play, *Lady Windermere's Fan*, was written towards the end of 1891 on the commission of George Alexander, the director of the Princess Theatre, and it received its first performance in February, 1892. It was a huge success with its West End audiences, though the critics were a little more cautious in their response. While they tended to agree that the play was brilliantly written, with some of the finest dialogue they had ever heard, they were rather dubious about the melodramatic nature of the plot which, they argued, was commonplace and tedious. The anonymous critic of the *Daily Telegraph*, for 22 February 1892, for example, attacked the plot as creaking, and concluded:

> The play is a bad one, but it will succeed. No faults in construction, no failure in interest, no feebleness in character drawing, no staleness in motive, will weigh in the scale against the insolence of its caricature. Society loves best those who chaff it most, and society will rush to see Lady Windermere, and cringe to be tickled by her fan.
>
> (Tydeman 1982: 48)

And William Archer, an extremely influential critic of the period, a man who collaborated with George Bernard Shaw, and championed the experimental works of Henrik Ibsen, castigated the play for its psychological improbabilities. He suggests that Lord Windermere is acting stupidly in his relationship with the scheming Mrs Erlynne; and that Mrs Erlynne herself is built up on a contradiction, though in the end he doesn't dislike her character because her complexity or doubleness lifts her out of the realms of melodrama. However, in an article in *World* for 24 February 1892, he wrote of his disquiet about the inconsistent characterization of the title character:

> The fatal inconsistency is in the character of Lady Windermere. In the first act, at five p.m., she is a woman carved in alabaster, from whom, in her own conceit, all possible soilure seems infinitely remote. . . . She is a happy wife and mother, without even the dimmest suspicion of her husband's faith. . . . Yet this very woman, seven hours later, is prepared to abandon her child without a thought (does Mr. Wilde wish us to believe that she actually forgets its existence?) and then to throw herself into the arms of a man for whom she feels nothing but a very unimpassioned friendship. When Lord Darlington began to make love to Lady Windermere in the ball room, I wondered at what seemed to me his tactless and self-defeating precipitancy; when Lady Windermere for a moment listened to him, I could not believe my ears; when she went off to join him, I pinched myself to make sure that I was not dreaming. . . . If Lady Windermere had set to work to swear like a trooper and smash the furniture, her conduct would have been just as rational, and not a whit more improbable.
>
> (Tydeman 1982: 49–50)

This is overstatement and possibly misses the point of Lady Windermere's behaviour. In this play, as in the later *Ideal Husband*, the ideal woman has inhabited too literally the standards of her society. In her disappointment with her husband, she attempts to enact the only revenge open to her: to match his perceived adultery with an adulterous liaison of her own. The play significantly has the subtitle 'A Play about a Good Woman', and its central action is concerned with how good and bad – in men and women – is to be defined. By implication, it mounts a critique of the sexual double standard, which demands sexual chastity in women, but which nods at indiscretions and worse in men. As the curtain rises, Lady Windermere establishes herself as a moral absolutist. She tells Lord Darlington of the certainty of her own moral principles:

> You think I am a Puritan I suppose? Well, I have something of the Puritan in me. I was brought up like that. I am glad of it. My mother died when I was a mere child. I lived always with Lady Julia, my father's elder sister, you know. She was stern to me, but she taught me what the world is forgetting, the difference that there is between right and wrong. *She* allowed of no compromise. *I* allow of none . . . . Nowadays people seem to look on life as a speculation. It is not a speculation. It is a sacrament. Its ideal is Love. Its purification is Sacrifice.
>
> (CW: 422, original emphasis)

She speaks as a figure whose world view has been constructed out of the Old Testament version of a God of Vengeance, telling her husband when he asks her to invite Mrs Erlynne to her party: 'If a woman really repents, she never wishes to return to the society that has made or seen her ruin' (CW: 430). Lady Windermere has these principles so firmly in place, the play implies, because she has never been tested. They are principles without substance (and, of course the supreme dramatic irony of the play is that it is in the end Mrs Erlynne, the fallen woman, who lives out the ideal of life as Love and Sacrifice, and who does so without any of the moral cant that her daughter spouts).

The journey she goes on through the play is a series of lessons in moral relativism. Even at the beginning of the play, one might argue, her principles are compromised by her permitting Lord Darlington to visit at all. She may say that she dislikes his extravagant compliments, but she still allows him to come to her house to pay them. For his own purposes, of course, Darlington is keen to teach Lady Windermere an alternative moral code – for, if she were not an absolutist, she might consider running away with him. In a veiled way, he puts to her the hypothetical situation that her husband is unfaithful, and tries to suggest that if she were thus mistreated, she would be entitled to 'console herself'. When she responds in terms of her principles to that hypothesis, he comments to her: 'Do you know I am afraid that good people do a great deal of harm in this world. Certainly the greatest harm they do is that they make badness of such extraordinary

importance' (CW: 423). Moreover, the most hurtful thing she says
to Mrs Erlynne is: 'Women like you have no hearts. . . . You are
bought and sold' (CW: 447) – an accusation of prostitution in all
but name: but she forgets herself that her beautiful house in Covent
Garden and the estate at Selby, the lifestyle she leads, and the clothes
on her back, are also 'bought and sold', the only difference between
her own legitimacy and Mrs Erlynne's wickedness is her marriage
certificate. Lady Windermere has to learn that in morality there is no
simple equivalence of black and white. Instead, the world operates
in multiple shades of grey. A 'bad' person can commit a good act;
and Lady Windermere's own goodness is compromised by her flight
to Lord Darlington's rooms after the ball. As yet, she has, of course
done nothing; but she learns from that moment that the appearance
of goodness may be at least as important as its actuality. At the end
of the play, she achieves consciousness of Mrs Erlynne's goodness; but
she remains unself-conscious about the possible moral dubiousness
of her own position.

If Lady Windermere is a prig, her husband is a fool. He cannot
see that his own position is hopelessly compromised by his financial
and social arrangements with Mrs Erlynne. To anyone who does not
know the truth (and of course the audience does not discover the
truth until nearly at the end of Act 4), there is only one construction
to put on their relationship: it must be that of lover and mistress. The
only interesting and complex figure in the text is Mrs Erlynne herself,
which is ironic since in many ways she is a figure directly out of melodrama, whose story is the stock story – the young bride, seduced away
from her proper sphere, her husband and daughter, by a dastardly
lover. The public nature of the scandal of her life makes it impossible
for her to frequent polite society – though, as the play shows, that
society is not quite so lily-white as it would like to pretend itself to be
(as witnessed, for example by Lady Plymdale's injunction to Dumby
– her lover perhaps? – to introduce her husband to Mrs Erlynne). In
melodrama and sensation fiction, the fallen woman suffers the fate
that Lady Windermere assumes should be Mrs Erlynne's fate – igno-
miny and silent repentance. As Mrs Erlynne says to Lord Windermere
towards the end of the play:

> I suppose, Windermere, you would like me to retire into a convent,
> or become a hospital nurse, or something of that kind, as people do

in silly modern novels. That is stupid of you, Arthur; in real life, we don't do such things – not as long as we have any good looks left, at any rate. No – what consoles one nowadays is not repentance but pleasure. Repentance is quite out of date. And besides, if a woman really repents, she has to go to a bad dressmaker, otherwise no one believes in her. And nothing in the world would induce me to do that.

(CW: 460)

Wilde's message here is that repentance is reduced to a performance, complete with costume changes.

If Mrs Erlynne is the stock character from Victorian melodrama, the wicked adventuress with a line in blackmail and a sexual past, she also stakes a claim for her own reality and roundedness as a character. She will not act out the part that melodramatic convention assigns to her for her ending, even if she is prepared, in the midst of the drama, to take on the role of self-sacrificing mamma for the sake of her daughter. She is an interesting and original character because she refuses the categorisation that her morality and the melodramatic genre seems to demand of her: she is at once, an adventurer, an adulteress, a blackmailer, a mother, an idealist – and, despite being a woman with a past, she is also, at the end of the play, a woman with a future, married to the infinitely malleable Augustus (Tuppy) Lorton, whose nickname marks him out as a future cuckold. Melodrama is supposed to take place in terms of moral absolutism – you cheer the dashing hero and fainting heroine, hiss the moustache-twirling villain. Reality does not, of course, make those interpretations nearly so easy for the viewer. And this is compounded by the fact that Mrs Erlynne has most of the best lines. Her only punishment for her immorality is the painful emotion that maternity calls out from her, and it is a painful emotion that she has no intention of repeating:

Oh, don't imagine I am going to have a pathetic scene with [my daughter], weep on her neck and tell her who I am, and all that kind of thing. *I have no ambition to play the part of a mother.* Only once in my life have I known a mother's feelings. That was last night. They were terrible – they made me suffer – they made me suffer too much. For twenty years, as you say, I have lived childless – I want to live childless still. (*Hiding her feelings with a trivial laugh.*) Besides, my dear Windermere, how on earth could I *pose* as a mother with a grown-up

daughter? Margaret is twenty-one, and I have never admitted that I
am more than twenty-nine, or thirty at the most. Twenty-nine when
there are pink shades, thirty when there are not.

(CW: 460, my emphases)

Mrs Erlynne's mixed genre is very clear in that speech – she is simultaneously the melodrama mother and the melodrama adventuress
with a line in cynical humour. At the end of the play, her relationship
with Lady Windermere is not made clear to her daughter.

The play turns on the prop of the fan, a gift from husband to wife
on the occasion of her coming of age. The fan starts as evidence of
affection between husband and wife; it becomes a potential weapon
when Lady Windermere threatens to strike Mrs Erlynne with it; it
becomes a piece of incriminating evidence about Lady Windermere's
intentions with Lord Darlington; and finally it is the unknowing gift
between mother and daughter who share – significantly perhaps – the
same name, implying that they are made of the same stuff, and that
they might have shared the same fate (Mrs Erlynne acts, she says, to
stop history from repeating itself). The sign of Lady Windermere's
new found maturity is her ability to accept moral relativity; but the
fan is also a sign of her immaturity and her commodity status. She
may be of age, but she's still too young to know who her mother is.
Both husband and mother treat her like a child.

The play uses elements of realism in order to complicate ideas
about morality; and uses elements of melodrama to complicate a
common-sense nineteenth-century version of reality. Wilde strug-
gles with the tensions between the representation of reality and the
imperative of the theatrical space to be dramatic – that is, unrealistic.
In modern-dress dramas, there was a move towards what has come to
be called fourth-wall drama, sometimes known in the period as the
'well-made play' in which the action is set in a solidly realized room
(with wallpaper, particular kinds of furniture, very realistic props
and so forth), and the audience, which is never acknowledged by the
players, makes up the fourth wall of the room.

In part, and ironically, given all Wilde had to say about realism
in essays such as 'The Decay of Lying', his society comedies in part
buy into the process of realism. The setting of *Lady Windermere*, for
example, demands very specific elements about what is in each of the
rooms, and where the doors for entrance and exit are. The time is set

as 'the present.' There is a sense in which he was 'holding the mirror' up to his audience, representing their own domestic spaces and their own morals and attitudes on play before them. What is really striking about Wilde's plays is that for all their apparent 'realism', what he really points out is the artificial nature of the real and the natural. The dialogue, for example, is spoken with a fluency or wit that is entirely unreal: no-one (except perhaps Wilde himself) really spoke like this. Sentiments are expressed which polite society cannot stomach. The reality of the setting is at odds with the polish of the language and improbabilities of both plot and characterization. In other words, as Wilde often did, he is using the conventions of the genre in which he writes against themselves for comic and satirical purpose. This is also a function of genre. The drawing room comedy of manners is a form which focuses on *codes* of behaviour among a social elite. The code of behaviour matters more than the morality that it is meant to represent.

The play combines elements of plot with elements of social commentary, which rebound largely on the minor characters, are spoken and dramatized by them. Of the major characters, only Mrs Erlynne consistently comments on the social scene in a critical way; the Windermeres, and even Lord Darlington to some extent, are too much part of the social scene to make sense of its faults. As with the essays 'The Decay of Lying' and 'The Critic as Artist', the social satire depends on the inversion of expected values in such a way as to expose the fact that society, for all its pretence of virtue, is actually founded on hypocrisy and vice. The satire depends very largely on nineteenth-century gender stereotypes (something that is replicated in *The Importance of Being Earnest*). The middle- or upper-class woman was assumed to be chaste, demure, dependent, maternal and ignorant of the seamier side of life. The middle- or upper-class man, on the other hand, was assumed to be a 'man of the world'; he was expected to have a knowledge of life's unpleasantness – though, in his ideal form, he would also disapprove of immorality and unchastity. What *Lady Windermere's Fan* dramatizes is that these stereotypes are not firm or stable. In his objection to the contradictory psychology of Lady Windermere, William Archer, in the passage quoted above, was explicitly referring to the stereotype of the 'good woman', fixed firmly in her goodness; and he objected to the possibility that she might develop in other directions. The social world that Wilde presents demonstrates the fluidity of gender values – and, by extension, the fluidity of the moral systems which support them.

In the minor characters such as Augustus (Tuppy) Lorton, we see 'a man of the world' whose marker of experience is that he has been 'twice married and once divorced, or twice divorced and once married' – Cecil Graham can't quite remember which, a forgetfulness that trivializes marriage in a somewhat shocking way (CW: 435). But whatever the truth of his experience, it has taught Tuppy nothing: experience is merely the name he gives to his mistakes, but there is no sense that he will not repeat the same mistakes at the end in his projected marriage to Mrs Erlynne. Similarly, a character like Dumby shows that the experience of masculinity is passive rather than active. He may criticise Tuppy's passivity in the face of Mrs Erlynne's charms, but he appears to be very much under the thumb of Lady Plymdale. He comments in Lord Darlington's rooms that 'It is perfectly brutal the way most women nowadays behave to men who are not their husbands' (CW: 450), but he cannot take his own advice. Of all the men with speaking parts (except for the butler, Parker), the only one who is entirely disengaged from the sex war implicit in this society's machinations is Cecil Graham who says cynical things and acts not at all (surely an interesting thing in a drama to find a character who does nothing 'dramatic', but particularly significant in a context where masculinity is itself defined by action). When Lord Darlington comments on the cynicism of his friends – he is, after all, in love, and therefore not cynical, Graham asks him:

> Cecil Graham. What is a cynic?
> Lord Darlington. A man who knows the price of everything and the value of nothing.
> Cecil Graham. And a sentimentalist, my dear Darlington, is a man who sees an absurd value in everything, and doesn't know the market price of any single thing.
>
> (CW: 452)

It is Darlington's definition of cynicism that has passed into the public consciousness, but Graham's definition is in fact much more cynical. Darlington comments that Graham talks like a man of experience, but it is clear that Graham *only* talks: he talks so much that he never has any experiences of his own. He is passive in the face of the social world and thus is easily manipulated by Mrs Erlynne into introducing her to his very respectable aunt, Lady Jedburgh.

Against the alleged experience of men, there is the innocence and passivity of women. This is viciously satirized in the figures of Lady Agatha Carlisle (the duchess of Berwick's daughter), whose words – and, it is implied, her entire experience – are limited to compliance to her mother's will: she only ever says 'yes, mamma'. Her innocence is apparently absolute, though one might play her as a more scheming figure in the episode where her mother discovers that she has consented to live in Australia after her marriage – as if the daughter seeks to escape the will of the mother on the other side of the world. Agatha's passivity is repeated sevenfold in the figure of Miss Graham, Lady Jedburgh's niece (and Cecil's sister perhaps), who never speaks at all, but merely silently follows her aunt around the stage.

Set against these powerless women who perfectly represent and parody the stereotype of ideal, silent femininity, are the figures of the main plot – Lady Windermere, who at least thinks that she knows her own mind, and more importantly Mrs Erlynne. Lady Windermere may appear like a 'good' woman, but her conception of goodness narrows her version of reality into something impossible. With Mrs Erlynne, however, one sees a woman who has arrogated masculine powers and privileges to herself: her sexual past, and her machinations for a financially secure future, are supposedly the works of the masculine mind. And one is left to wonder which is the more positive role model at the end of the play – the good women like Lady Agatha or Miss Graham, or the wicked woman who takes such firm control over her own destiny?

The world in which the play is set is an artificial world which pretends that it is natural. Wilde is laughing at the very society that is paying good money to come to the theatre to see his play, and gently demonstrating that their own positions are nothing but ideological constructions of reality. The satire does not foment rebellion, but it does undercut the idea that the current organization of society is reasonable. Like Hardy's *Tess of the D'Urbervilles*, subtitled *A Pure Woman*, this play has a subtitle that subverts the ideal that goodness is easily identified and morally absolute. The opposing figures of Lady Windermere and Mrs Erlynne are both awarded the title of 'goodness'. Traditionally, they should be seen as moral opposites, but the concept of goodness has been collapsed to make both of them fit it:

'a truth in art is that whose contradictory is also true' (CW: 1173). As Regenia Gagnier has put it, the play is double-edged; it operates between two interpretations, the cynical and the sentimental, and it refuses the categorization of people in terms of sterile moral oppositions: 'The play could have been called the unimportance of being Margaret, the unimportance of being Mother, or indeed, the unimportance of being married' (Gagnier 1986: 117–19). In order to parody the ideal or the stereotype, a text must first invoke it, This parodic strategy enable Wilde at once to attack and to mock his audiences and their preconceptions.

Artificial Worlds:
Salomé *and* The Importance of Being Earnest

The world of the social comedy may superficially look 'real', but it is not real or natural at all. It is a world that depends absolutely on artifice, and it suggests that the real world it represents is equally artificial. As a form, it is also concerned, in Wilde's hands, much more with language than with action, and the point about the language is that it is not 'effective' in that it bears no steady relationship with the reality it is alleged to describe. As comments on *Lady Windermere* above might start to hint, language does not perform its normal functions in Wilde's plays in two distinct ways. First, the words that are associated with high moral values are repeatedly shown to be empty signifiers. What, after all, does 'good' mean if it is applied equally to the innocent (if slightly obnoxious) ingénue, Lady Windemere, and to her 'guilty' adventuring mother, Mrs Erlynne? In other words, in Wilde's writing there is often an assault on the standards that language is supposed to help his rigid society to uphold. Secondly, on a more micro level, one can also see repeatedly that language is ineffective in its relation to day-to-day action. The girl, Agatha, who repeats the single phrase, 'Yes, Mamma', in apparent obedience to her mother's iron will (Lady Bracknell should be so lucky with her own daughter), is very much the exception. In both *Salomé* and *Earnest*, language is the medium of play, but it is also the medium by which the play's action is baffled. In two very different contexts, Wilde mounts an assault on a common-sense view of the relationships between words and the world, and in doing so, steps beyond the simple 'realism' of his age and looks forward to the experimental dramas of modernism.

Salomé is very different from Wilde's other forays into dramatic art in the 1890s, at least at first sight. We are no longer in the natural-seeming, though nonetheless artificial, world of contemporary society, but in the biblical world of Herod Antipas, Israel at the time of Christ and John the Baptist. It is a highly experimental drama, and it has seldom found a commercial audience, particularly because Wilde is so much associated with epigrammatic wit, and this play appears on the surface to have very little that is 'typically Wildean' about it. The play does, however, make use of the same themes that one finds in Wilde's comedies – in particular the relationships between masculinity and femininity – only on this occasion, he does so as tragedy rather than as comedy, though there are certainly incongruously comic moments in his biblical play. He wrote to an unnamed correspondent in 1894:

> Whether a comedy should deal with modern life, whether its subject should be society or middle-class existence, these are questions purely to the artist's own choice. Personally, I like comedy to be intensely modern, and like my tragedy to walk in purple and to be remote: but these are whims merely.
>
> (Ellmann 1988: 321)

It may be a whim, but it expresses Wilde's sense that the 'earnestness' of the nineteenth century is actually very funny; it allows him to mock what some would have regarded as the serious, and to make tragedy out of the long ago and far away.

The biblical figure of Salomé was in vogue in late-nineteenth-century art and literature. The biblical account of her story is vague, but gave enough material to inspire many versions of her. Its lack of specificity allowed each artist to create his own version of her. As Bram Dijkstra has argued, she was *the* figure of the *femme fatale* for the period, a fruitful image because she combined a louche sexual attractiveness (she was a belly dancer associated with nakedness) with a fatality that directly attacked institutional religion – her role in the decapitation of John the Baptist. She combined a powerful (and therefore unfeminine) sexuality with an exotic artistic potential, and a rewriting of the masculine values of patriarchal Judaeo-Christian religion. 'In the turn of the century imagination,' writes Dijkstra, 'the figure of Salomé epitomized the perversity of women: their eternal circularity and their ability to destroy the male's soul even while they remained nominally chaste in body' (Dijkstra 1986: 384). For the late nineteenth century, the biblical account of Salomé had enormous potency. It is a story about cruelty, about the usurpation of a king's power through the agency of his own sexual weakness, and it is set in the exotic (and therefore erotic) location of long ago and far away. As early as the 1870s, the paintings of the subject by Gustave Moreau began to appear. What attracted Moreau to Salomé was the opportunity to depict the highly sexualized image of the female body, and the exotic location of Herod's court, both of which gave him a freedom that contemporary concerns with realistic art would have disallowed. His decor is lavish, and his Salomé is sexy – he could never have painted a contemporary woman quite like that. Painters and writers followed his lead. In particular, Gustave Flaubert wrote his own version of the story, entitled 'Herodias' (in *Trois Contes*, 1877) and Des Esseintes, the hero of Joris-Karl Huysmans's *A Rebours* (1884, the novel which allegedly corrupts Dorian Gray) owns copies of Moreau's pictures. Wilde possibly got the idea of writing his own staged version from a meeting early in 1891 with the French poet Stéphane Mallarmé, who was then engaged in writing his own version, *Hérodiade* (a poem begun in 1860s and which was still incomplete at his death). It offered him, as it offered his contemporaries and predecessors, an infinitely malleable image of wicked femininity.

Wilde may also have been attracted by the fact that Salomé is a dancer – a figure who dramatizes the decadent concern we established with combining art and life. As W. B. Yeats was to put it 30 years later in his poem 'Among Schoolchildren': 'How can we know the dancer from the dance?' As Frank Kermode has established in his 1957 book *Romantic Image*, the dancer was considered as the perfect example of the organic image, in which there can be no separation between form and content. Kermode suggests that Wilde was influenced by Moreau's paintings, and by the versions of Salomé produced in French culture by Maeterlinck, Flaubert and Mallarmé. But what he says that differentiates Wilde's Salomé from earlier versions is that she, unlike them, knows her own mind. Wilde's version of the story, that is, does not just see the dancer as a sexy figure who is unaware of her own attractions, and who acts on the instruction of her mother; rather, his Salomé acts out her own desires and fantasies, and the responsibility for the death of John the Baptist is hers rather than Herodias's. She explicitly states: 'I do not heed my mother. It is for mine own pleasure that I ask the head of Jokanaan in a silver charger' (CW: 600) So Wilde's version transforms the story from its origins in vagueness, and from its contemporary representations as a story of motives of jealousy on the part of the mother to a allegory of sexual power and the ways in which such power can be abused.

Perhaps in homage to his French masters, Wilde wrote the play in French during the last months of 1891. After a series of quarrels, it was eventually translated into English by Lord Alfred Douglas (this is the translation we still use today, and it is not entirely accurate), and was published in this English translation with illustrations by Aubrey Beardsley in 1894. Beardsley made himself the obvious person to illustrate the English edition of the play by advertising his interest in it with an illustration in *Studio* magazine in 1893 (the French edition of the play appeared that year). His illustrative style was one that spoke to Wilde, particularly in its deliberate emphasis of form over content, and his distortions of the conventions of realist perspective in his drawings. His most famous works, including the illustrations for *Salomé* are all black and white line drawings, with no half-tones to suggest the depth of three dimensions. He frequently plays tricks with perspective, and he emphasizes line and surface rather than mimetic representation. With a schoolboyish glee, he also tended to concentrate on macabre subject matter, often hiding perverse and obscene images in seemingly innocent drawings. Beardsley drew, as Wilde wrote, for two different audiences: for those who simply saw the surface and for those who interpreted more dubious meanings. Wilde was attracted to Beardsley's drawings and stylized forms. In the edition of *Salomé* he sent to Beardsley, he wrote: 'For Aubrey: for the only artist beside myself who knows what the dance of the seven veils is, and can see that invisible dance' (CL: 578n), signalling that it was the interpretation of what could not be directly stated that he valued most in the artist's work. In the event, Beardsley had some difficulty in fulfilling the commission, in part owing to the fact that John Lane, the publisher, was very nervous about the drawings, fearing a prosecution for obscenity. The original drawing Beardsley produced entitled 'The Toilette of Salomé', for instance, was vetoed by Lane, who objected to the depiction of a naked page in a corner of the drawing, who had very visible pubic hair, something that Victorian culture had radically excluded from its conventions of representation of the naked human form. And Beardsley continued to do slightly 'naughty' things in his pictures; for instance, piling up 'forbidden' books such as Zola's *La Terre*, and Charles Baudelaire's *Les fleurs du mal* (both texts that had been prosecuted for obscenity) on Salomé's dressing table.

As the remark about Salomé's dressing table might suggest, strictly speaking, Beardsley did not illustrate Wilde's text. He refused to subordinate his productions to the text, and he illustrated scenes that the play does not contain. Moreover, he broke the rules of illustration in the sense that his depictions of recurrent character – Salomé herself for instance – would not be recognizable from one image to the next. What Beardsley seems to have realized is that in this play, each character is locked into an entirely subjective interpretation of the world. His pictures are, therefore, not only an interpretation (rather than a straightforward representation) of Wilde's script, but are also a creative critical commentary on it – something Wilde, at least in theory, would have approved. And like Wilde's writings, the illustrations push at the boundaries of what it is acceptable to represent at all, particularly in relation to explicitly sexual material. Wilde, I have suggested, sometimes wrote in 'code'; Beardsley drew in code, often displacing sexual content to the margins of his pictures (naked pages and grotesques in states of arousal, as in the picture 'The Eyes of Herod', or in the same picture, the multiple phallic symbols that surround the lustful monarch). The illicit is present, but disguised, and the viewer does not have to see if he or she chooses not to.

Wilde's intention was that the play would be performed in London with the French actress Sarah Bernhardt in the leading role. This plan was scuppered by the Lord Chamberlain's office (the censorship of plays was a throwback to the Stuart stage), which ruled that the play could not be performed in public because it depicted biblical characters. It was denied a performance licence, and did not receive its premiere until 1896, in Paris, when, of course, Wilde was already in prison. It was only performed for the first time in England in a private performance in 1916, when it became the subject of a prolonged and acrimonious court case, documented by Michael Hoare's book *Wilde's Last Stand*. (The leading actress, Maud Allan, sued the Tory MP, Noel Pemberton Billing, for libel after he described her production under the headline 'The Cult of the Clitoris'. Allan lost the case on the rather flimsy grounds that if she knew what a clitoris was, then she was obviously a lesbian, and did not deserve to have her reputation protected by the law.) The large format book published by Elkin Matthews and John Lane at the Bodley Head was also the subject of censorship on the grounds that some of Aubrey Beardsley's illustrations for the edition could be construed as obscene, and a number of them were suppressed before the book went to print.

The world created by Wilde in the play is one in which none of the normal rules of everyday reality apply – linguistic rules and rules of sexual behaviour are both regularly flouted. It opens, for example, with an encounter between two men, the Young Syrian and Herodias's Page:

> Young Syrian: How beautiful is the Princess Salomé tonight!
> Page of Herodias: Look at the moon! How strange the moon seems! She is like a woman rising from a tomb. She is like a dead woman. You would fancy she was looking for dead things.
> Syrian: She has a strange look. She is like a little princess who wears a yellow veil and whose feet are of silver. She is like a princess who has little white doves for feet. You would fancy she was dancing.
> Page: She is like a woman who is dead. She moves very slowly.
>
> (CW: 583)

In this passage there is, intentionally, some difficulty in establishing who/what the two young men are describing – what is the signified by the word 'she'? For one, it is the moon, for the other, the princess Salomé. This is a confusion that Salomé herself picks up when she enters the scene, and identifies herself with the moon; indeed, when Herod enters, he notices the moon – but he could just as easily be talking about his step-daughter:

> The moon has a strange look tonight. Has she not a strange look? She is like a mad woman, a mad woman who is seeking everywhere for lovers. She is naked too. She is quite naked. . . . She shows herself naked in the sky. She reels through the clouds like a drunken woman. Does she not reel like a drunken woman? She is like a mad woman, is she not?
>
> (CW: 592)

To which Herodias, ever mindful of the common-sense world of reality, retorts that 'the moon is just the moon, nothing else'.

There are several points that are made by this series of interpretations of the moon. *Salomé* is a play about the multiplicity of
significance, and the failure of any single fixed point of view to give
an adequate interpretation of the world. Like the Wildean work of art,
the moon is what each person sees in it, and what each person sees is
a measure of their own personality ('the highest as the lowest form of
criticism is a mode of autobiography', as Wilde has it in the Preface
to *Dorian Gray*). The young Syrian soldier associates the moon with
Salomé with whom he is hopelessly in love; he sees in the moon a
beautiful young woman. The page, whose own love for the Syrian
soldier is threatened by this interpretation, sees the moon as a fatal
or dead woman – a *femme fatale* with deathly significance. Salomé
sees the moon as cold, virginal and chaste: a goddess whose sexual
powers have 'never been defiled by a man', she says. For her, the moon
is self-contained and powerful. Herod, a dissolute and incestuous
monarch, sees a drunken naked woman in the moon – the sign of his
depraved sexuality and symptom of his impotent guilt. And Herodias
sees 'just the moon'.

Failures of interpretation proliferate throughout the play, in a
series of encounters where words are repeatedly misheard, ignored
or misunderstood. Instructions and orders are only obeyed in the
final fatal moments, when Herod orders the deaths of Iokanaan and
of Salomé herself. Elsewhere in the play, characters repeatedly tell
others to do or not to do a particular thing, and their interlocutor
ignores the words completely. Beginning with the young page's wish
that the Syrian captain not look at Salomé – 'You must not look at
her. You look too much at her' (CW: 584) – and moving through the
multiple refusals of Salomé to do the Tetrarch's bidding – 'I have no
desire to dance, Tetrarch' (CW: 597), and her mother's instructions to
her husband not to look at her daughter ('You must not look at her'
(CW: 596)), all of these instructions are disobeyed. As Herod says in
despair, when his step-daughter demands Iokanaan's head: 'You are
not listening. You are not listening' (CW: 601). The language is jewelled, but intransitive and ineffective, having no effect in the world.
This failure of language to communicate is particularly marked in
Salomé's encounter with Iokanaan, in which she speaks to him in both
the language of desire and the language of disgust, but in neither case
does the prophet respond in terms of what she actually says. Thus,
describing his beauty, in an aggressive and unfeminine expression of

desire (which is also, by the bye, the perfect excuse to linger on male beauty without seeming to do so perversely, a neat trick on the part of the playwright), Salomé produces a blazon of his attributes, using the listing effects that are usually reserved for descriptions of women's appearance in chivalric verse to define his attractions:

> I am amorous of your body! Thy body is white like the lilies of a field that a mower hath never mowed. Thy body is white like the snows that lie on the mountains, like the snows that lie on the mountains of Judaea, and come down into the valleys. The roses in the garden of the Queen of Arabia are not so white as thy body.
>
> (CW 589)

But when he rejects her approaches and refuses her looks ('I will not have her look at me'), his body becomes in her eyes 'hideous. It is like the body of a leper. It is like a plastered wall where vipers have crawled . . . it is like a whitened sepulchre full of loathsome things . . . thy body is horrible' (CW: 590). The same process of assertion and negation is repeated with Iokanaan's hair and mouth, focusing our attention on the sensuality of the princess. The proliferation of similes is an attempt to 'fix' the interpretation of the world and the characters; but it acts, paradoxically, to demonstrate that the words themselves are useless. As a seductress of Iokanaan, Salomé fails with her jewelled and metaphor-laden words. Only as the play turns to tragedy, with the executions of Iokanaan and the princess, does language become 'transitive', or effective. Realism – the relationship between the word and the world rendered transparent – is fatal in this play.

This is a world away from the trivial comedy, as Wilde called it, of *The Importance of Being Earnest*, but the thematic concern with language's intransigence and failure to communicate is played out here as well, though this time for comic effect. When the play opened on 14 February 1895, William Archer, who had been less impressed with *Lady Windermere*, writing in *World* magazine, was utterly dazzled by it.

> It is delightful to see, it sends wave after wave of laughter curling and foaming around the theatre; but as a text for criticism it is barren and delusive. It is like a mirage oasis in the desert, grateful and comforting to the weary eye, but when you come up close to it, behold! it is

intangible, it eludes your grasp. What can a poor critic do with a play which raises no principle, whether of art or of morals, creates its own canons and conventions, and is nothing but an absolutely wilful expression of an irrepressibly witty personality? Mr Pater . . . has an essay on the tendency of art to verge towards, and merge in, the absolute art – music. He might have found an example in *The Importance of Being Earnest*.

(CH: 189–90)

This was typical of the praise for the play. The only dissenting voice among the critics was that of George Bernard Shaw, who had loved Wilde's earlier plays, but found this one lacking, for precisely the same reasons that Archer had praised it:

I cannot say that I greatly cared for *The Importance of Being Earnest*. It amused me, of course; but unless comedy touches me as well as amuses me, it leaves me with the sense of having wasted my evening. I go to the theatre to be moved to laughter, not to be tickled or bustled into it.

(CH: 195)

What Shaw seems to have objected to is precisely what Archer praised – that the play raised no 'principles' whether or morality or of art. It is not, on the face of it, a political or moral drama; it eschews the melodramatic plot, which is at the heart of Wilde's earlier comedies, and concentrates, apparently, on pure farce without serious intention. It is a play at once at the very heart of the establishment; and simultaneously, it is also a play which speaks of sexually dissident meanings. Its apparently trivial form is, in fact, a kind of subversion of dominant models of gender and sexuality, but the subversion is played out in the language in which the action (such as it is) takes place.

Like the playwright, and like its male characters, Jack and Algy, *Earnest* leads a double life. Wilde, as we know, was on the one hand, a respectably married man, loving father, popular dinner guest and successful writer; on the other, he was a cynical rich man who enjoyed the company of young men, was not above paying them for the social and sexual services, and was, in turn, blackmailed for the privilege. He had a respectable face and a less respectable underbelly. As Ellmann says of Wilde, when faced with contradictory choices, he habitually chose them both. Camp is the mode that makes this possible.

From the title onwards, what is immediately signalled is that the serious, the important, the sincere and the earnest are present in the play, but that they are present entirely for the purpose of satire. The adjective 'earnest' is clearly a pun, a play on the proper name Ernest – suggesting that there should be a link between the two, Ernest by name, earnest by nature. When a serious concept like earnestness is placed in the context of a pun, it is clear that the concept itself is being debunked, and since 'earnestness' was a key marker of Victorian dominant ideology – and in particular, that earnestness marked out what it meant to be a proper man – a kind of dissidence against that norm is articulated by the play. It subverts not only Victorian conventions of behaviour, where 'real men' are earnest, but also Victorian conventions of representation. Names, after all, are important markers in fictions and on the stage. Novelists and playwrights do not generally choose the names of their characters at random. Here, the straightforward honesty of the name Ernest is being sent up. Both Jack Worthing and Algy Moncrieff appropriate the name that signals honesty in order to deceive. A name that is founded on the concept of truth becomes, in this case, a lie, a forgery, a counterfeit. Appearances are deceptive. Both Cecily Cardew and Gwendolen Fairfax fall in love with the name. In almost identical words they tell their respective suitors: 'My ideal has always been to love someone with the name of Ernest. There is something in the name that inspires absolute confidence. The moment Algernon first mentioned to me that he had a friend called Ernest, I knew I was destined to love you.' Cecily even becomes engaged to be married to the name before she has even met its putative owner. The play dramatizes an absolute separation between signifier and signified. In the first scene of the play, Algy tells Jack that 'The truth is never pure and rarely simple.' Language, which is the only medium in which truth can be expressed, distorts rather than mimetically represents the real.

Plays on language are essential throughout *Earnest*, as they are throughout Wilde's works. The critic Ernest Newman, writing in the *Free Review* in June 1895 (it is an exceptionally kind commentary given that Wilde was by this time already in prison), wrote of Wilde's use of non-referential language in his puns, epigrams and paradoxes, all of which call into question the relationship between language and truth. Newman wrote:

> The function of paradox is really the same as the function of religion
> – not to be believed; but the Philistine takes the one as seriously as
> he takes the other. A paradox is simply the truth of the minority,
> just as a commonplace is the truth of the majority. The function of
> paradox is to illumine light places, to explain just those things that
> everyone understands. For example, everyone knows what Art is, and
> everyone knows what it is to be immoral; but if a thinker says 'Art
> is immoral', the new synthesis puzzles them, and they either call it a
> paradox, or they say that the writer is immoral. In reality, he is doing
> just what they cannot do; he can see round corners, and the other
> side of things. Nay, he can do more than this; he can give to ordinary
> things a quality they have not. . . . We ordinary beings see objects
> in three dimensions only; a good paradox is a view in the fourth
> dimension.
>
> (CH: 203)

Paradox functions, that is, to break down the habitual, the conventional in thought. It displaces the things that everyone thought
they knew. As Pater said, failure is to form habits. On the small
scale of individual exchanges in the play, paradox produces only
laughter; but it has implications beyond itself. Once the audience
can be shaken out of habits in small things, they might also find
themselves shaken out of habits in larger things too. The paradox has
the potential to be deeply subversive.

In the play, the use of language marks out character. Attempts to
be sincere in the traditional use of the word are ruthlessly sent up.
Miss Prism and Canon Chasuble are romantically entwined; but
because of their observation of the conventional pieties of their day,
they can only declare their love in improbable metaphor. Their language practices take them as far as possible from the truths they are
trying to convey to each other about the state of their affections, and
they can only declare their love periphrastically:

> Were I fortunate enough to be Miss Prism's pupil, I would hang upon
> her lips. [*Miss Prism glares.*] I spoke metaphorically. My metaphor was
> drawn from the bees. Ahem.
>
> (CW: 377)

The metaphors (like the similes in *Salomé*) are hardly expressive of anything very much. Or again, in their discussion of marriage in the early church:

> Miss Prism. No married man is ever attractive except to his wife.
> Chasuble. And often, I have been told, not even to her.
> Miss Prism. That depends on the intellectual sympathies of the woman. Maturity can always be depended on. Ripeness can be trusted. Young women are green. [*Dr Chasuble starts.*] I spoke horticulturally. My metaphor was drawn from the fruits.
>
> (CW: 380)

The play is built up of conversation in which no-one ever precisely says what they mean. The plot should be the stuff of Victorian melodrama or sensation fiction, since it centres on a lost child's quest for his origins. Jack, indeed, explicitly refers to the genre of melodrama when he mistakenly identifies Miss Prism as 'Mother!', and is shocked to discover that he may be the child of an unmarried woman – though he is prepared to forgive her. But the plot is largely unimportant. It's not what is said that matters, but how it is said. And the point behind the dialogue is that it avoids the issue.

Characterization in the play depends not on individuality, not on people being unique and distinct, not on a notion of the deep structure of character which goes throughout a person's make up. The characters exist on the surface only and they are almost undifferentiated from each other. The speeches of Cecily and Gwendolen might easily be mixed up – Gwendolen is just a more sophisticated, citified version of Cecily; and Jack and Algy are often indistinguishable. The women, for example, both write diaries, which, although everything written in them is clearly a fabrication ('one must always have something sensational to read in the train', says Gwendolen), they both use as evidence to support their respective claims to be engaged to their non-existent suitor, Ernest Worthing. And the only essential difference between Algy and Jack is that Algy is greedier than Jack, and far more successful in satisfying his sensual lusts for cucumber sandwiches and muffins. Importantly, both men also lead double lives, leaving behind the responsibilities of their true positions in order to seek pleasure. The difference here is one of location: Jack, whose responsibilities are in the country, seeks his pleasure in the town; and Algy, who should be in town, seeks pleasure in the country.

Both are what Algy calls 'confirmed Bunburyists', a remark with a sly commitment to another phrase in the period, 'confirmed bachelor', with its connotations of a man who is not merely unmarried, but who prefers to remain so. There is a doubleness at the heart of *Earnest*, in which surface and depth speak at different times to different audiences who 'know' different things.

The first act exchange over Jack's lost cigarette case might be seen as a pure plot device, which allows Algy to learn of Jack's ward and his address in the country. But some members of the original audience would have known of another possible reading, and would have enjoyed a private joke at the expense of the rest of the audience. The fact that Jack and Algy smoke cigarettes at all in the 1890s might have been some indication to the original audience of a kind of effeminacy: the cigarette was the smoke of choice for the New Woman, not for the 'real man'. More importantly, Wilde's intimate circle would have known that the cigarette case was his preferred love token, the gift he habitually gave to his young male friends. Indeed, only two months later, cigarette cases inscribed with words of love would form part of the evidence against Wilde at his trials. No wonder then that Jack is horrified to discover that Algy has read the inscription in his case: 'It is a very ungentlemanly thing to do to read a private cigarette case,' he says. His fear is that he has been discovered leading a double life. But here, the cigarette case leads ironically to the discovery that Jack is actually more respectable than he would like to pretend to be. He behaves very well in the country – so the evidence of the cigarette case proves not his criminality, but his innocence. The audience with access to the code is given a choice about how to interpret the scene. We can read it aslant, or we can read it 'straight' – or, indeed, we can choose both and oscillate between the two.

Just as with 'The Critic as Artist', the places in which value is thought to reside are all inverted in the play through the playful use of language. Wilde takes the commonplace and upends it. During Lady Bracknell's quizzing of Jack about whether he is an eligible suitor for her daughter, the standard questions that might concern a properly engaged parent are up-ended. She is glad to hear that he smokes, 'since a man should always have an occupation of some kind.' She is happy that he knows nothing, since 'ignorance is a delicate exotic fruit', and she disapproves of anything that tampers with it. She asks the traditional questions about income and expectations, and is ironically pleased to hear that his income derives from investments rather than land – land has traditionally been regarded as the more assured basis for security. She discovers his extensive property, and is only concerned that his house in Belgrave Square is on the unfashionable side. She is pleased that he has no politics, being a Liberal Unionist (an Irish joke, which is about contradiction, since the Liberals were at this point in favour of Home Rule for the Irish). And his family is only a minor matter until the scene descends into farce with the discovery that Jack has been parented by an item of luggage:

> To be born, or at any rate, bred in a handbag, whether it had handles or not, seems to me to display a contempt for the ordinary decencies of family that reminds one of the worst excesses of the French Revolution. . . . As for the particular locality in which the handbag was found, a cloakroom at a railway station might serve to conceal a social indiscretion – has probably, indeed, used for that purpose before now – but it could hardly be regarded as an assured basis for a recognized position in good society. . . . You can hardly imagine that I and Lord Bracknell would dream of allowing our only daughter – a girl brought up with the utmost care – to marry into a cloakroom, and form an alliance with a parcel.
>
> (CW: 369–70)

The remarks about the cloakroom are heavily charged for those in the know. Then, as now, railway stations were often red-light districts for prostitutes of both sexes, and cloak rooms have a particular resonance as places in which illicit assignations might take place. But the real point here is that Lady Bracknell, the representative of moral rectitude and social awareness, does not care that her future son-in-law is an idle, smoking, ignorant layabout, so long as he is rich and has a better family background than a Gladstone bag. Her views on the role of masculinity are parroted by her daughter – in the Bracknell family, conventional gender roles are reversed – and Gwendolen says of her father:

> Outside the family circle, Papa, I am glad to say, is entirely unknown. I think that is quite as it should be. The home seems to me to be the proper sphere for the man. And certainly, once a man begins to neglect

his domestic duties, he becomes painfully effeminate, does he not? And I don't like that. It makes men so very attractive.

(CW: 397)

Jack, I think, is quite right to be worried that Gwendolen might turn out like her mother.

There are very few attempts in the play to be sincere and honest, and those that occur are treated with contempt. When Cecily and Gwendolen first meet, they agree to call each other by their Christian names, and then, to call each other sister. But when their disagreement over the ownership of the non-existent Ernest surfaces, as Cecily puts it, they 'cast aside the shallow mask of manners':

> Cecily. When I see a spade, I call it a spade.
> Gwendolen [*satirically*]. I am glad to say that I have never seen a spade. It is obvious to me that our social spheres have been widely different.

(CW: 399)

In his book *Sexual Dissidence*, Jonathan Dollimore reads this passage as typical of Wilde's language practice, in which an apparently simple reversal of values has more significance than that of the mere joke.

> Cecily tries to take over what we might call the high ground of the straightforward as opposed to the low ground of the shallow, the mannered and the duplicitous. . . . Gwendolen repudiates the implied opposition and kicks Cecily straight back into the domain of class, the 'social sphere'. Never has a spade been so effectively 'defamiliarized'. Compare Wilde's use of the same idea in May 1892, when an alderman had praised him for calling a spade a spade. Wilde replied: 'I would like to protest against the idea that I have ever called a spade a spade. The man who did so should be condemned to use one.'

(Dollimore 1991: 16–17)

For Wilde, language is always slippery, and its effects cannot be accurately predicted. Language practice in the above exchange implies that significance is defined by reception rather than by intention – words mean what the hearer wants them to mean, as opposed to the power of definition lying with the speaker. Cecily intends one result, and gets quite another. And it is a repeated structure of the play that language loses its meaning between utterance and reception. The characters are often found, therefore, effectively talking to themselves in an intransitive language.

Only Jack really takes language seriously; not a surprise, since his name is 'really' Ernest. When Algy tells him not to eat the cucumber sandwiches, Jack does not eat the cucumber sandwiches. Language acts transitively on him, making him act in certain ways. Part of the comedy arises out of his inability to see that the relationship between signifier and signified is irrelevant to everyone else. When Jack turns up at the country house in acted mourning for his fictional brother, only Miss Prism and Canon Chasuble take his clothes seriously. Cecily takes one look at them, and refuses to connect the form of mourning dress with its meaning:

> Uncle Jack! . . . What horrid clothes you have got on! Do go and change them. . . . What's the matter, Uncle Jack? You look as if you had toothache, and I have got such a surprise for you. Who do you think is in the dining room? Your brother! . . . He arrived about half an hour ago.
>
> (CW: 382–3)

Cecily already knows what her uncle will never know – that appearances and reality seldom match up. He is acting sadness, and looks like he has toothache; his costume is not read by her at all except as aesthetically displeasing.

Another example is Gwendolen and Cecily's tea when the two women are in suppressed fury with each other over their claims to Ernest, but cannot express their fury because of the presence of the servants. In the tea-table exchange, Gwendolen tries to do the naive thing and to connect language with action. She gives Cecily very strict instructions about the serving of her tea. Cecily decisively ignores those instructions, rendering them intransitive. Gwendolen might as well have been talking to herself. She shows her fury in her direct contradiction of her 'first impressions' of Cecily:

> You have filled my tea with lumps of sugar, and though I asked most decidedly for bread and butter, you have given me cake. I am known for the gentleness of my disposition, and the extraordinary sweetness

of my nature, but I warn you, Miss Cardew, you may go too far . . . .
From the moment I saw you, I distrusted you. I felt that you were
false and deceitful. I am never deceived in such matters. My first
impressions of people are invariably right.

(CW: 400)

In as much as the play is about anything, it is about the misuse of
language, and the failure of language to live up to its promise to make
sense of the world. In subverting the very medium through which
truth is supposed to be expressed, it opens up the possibility that the
entire basis of society is fake as well. Language operates as the medium
of truth – but it is also the place in which lies are told.

It is of course Jack, also to be known as Ernest, who is the bearer of
unwitting truth. He is an unsophisticated user of language, and does
not fully understand its potential for deception. When he is caught
out by the two girls in the lie of his brother's existence, he says:

It is very painful for me to be forced to speak the truth. It is the first
time in my life that I have been reduced to such a painful position,
and I am really quite inexperienced in doing anything of the kind.
However, I will tell you quite frankly, that I have no brother Ernest.
I have no brother at all. I have never had a brother in my life, and
I certainly have not the smallest intention of ever having one in the
future. . . . Not even of any kind.

(CW: 402)

Of course, though Jack intends to tell the truth, at this moment he
is still lying, though he does not know it yet. In this world, the truth
is rarely pure and never simple. It is certainly not an absolute value,
and the meaning of truth alters as the plot moves on. Jack Worthing,
indeed, has no brother, not even of any kind. But when Jack becomes
Ernest Moncrieff, he does have a brother – of sorts – and at the end
of the play he remarks:

Gwendolen, it is a terrible thing for a man to find out suddenly
that all his life he has been speaking nothing but the truth. Can you
forgive me?

(CW: 418)

At the end of the play, Jack says that he has learnt 'the vital importance of being earnest'. In fact, of course, he has learnt nothing of the kind. He may, as he says, have been speaking the truth all his life, but he had no intention of doing so – he intended to deceive, to lie, to separate the signifier from the signified. It is a moot point as to whether he has ever told the truth at all, since any traditional definition of truthfulness would be concerned with intention as well as performance; truth ought to be a function of sincerity (earnestness) rather than of accident or coincidence. This oscillation between value systems is the space of camp. It is incidentally extremely funny. It may also lead to acts of violence in Grosvenor Square: it is rebellious because it undoes the rules of the language game, laying bare its assumptions, and in the process it offers an experimental theatre in a context where the traditions all appear to be intact.

Chapter Six
Prison Writings

Who wants to be consistent? The dullard and the doctrinaire, the tedious people who carry out their principles to the bitter end of action, to the reductio ad absurdam of practice. Not I. Like Emerson, I write over the door of my library the word 'Whim'.

('The Decay of Lying', CW: 1072)

Even in actual life egotism is not without its attractions. When people talk to us about others, they are usually dull. When they talk to us about themselves, they are nearly always interesting, and if one could shut them up when they become wearisome as easily as one can shut up a book of which has grown wearied, they would be perfect absolutely. . . . Every great man nowadays has his disciples, and it is always Judas who writes the biography.

('The Critic as Artist', Part I, CW: 1109)

. . . it is of course necessary . . . to know oneself: that is the first achievement of knowledge. But to recognise that the soul of a man is unknowable, is the ultimate achievement of wisdom. The final mystery is oneself.

(*De Profundis*, CW: 1038)

As a writer, Wilde insisted on the multiplicity of interpretation and action, and refused totalizing explanations or moral systems throughout his work. In 'The Critic as Artist', he expressed his distrust for biographical writing because of its will to explain and totalize. Totalizing explanation, he suggests, is a mode of betrayal – Judas writes the biography – because it necessarily fictionalizes reality, and belies the complexity of the artist's self. Consistency and coherence are also to be avoided. 'Whim' is the keynote of the developed self. When Jack tells Gwendolen in *Earnest* that she is 'quite perfect', she responds: 'Oh, I hope I am not that. It would leave no room for developments, and I intend to develop in many directions' (CW: 363–4). As in all her exchanges with Jack, she gets the laugh line; the laughter is the sign in that play that she is right.

The text that we now know as *De Profundis* was written by Prisoner C.3.3., one Oscar Wilde, in Reading prison between January and March, 1897, in the form of a letter to Lord Alfred Douglas. Its status as a text is and was contested. As Josephine Guy and Ian Small suggest, it would be simplistic to see it purely as a letter to Douglas, though that was the 'pre-text' for its production. We know that Wilde wrote the text carefully, and that there is internal evidence that he made fair copy of parts of it while still in prison. On his release, he made careful arrangements for it to be typewritten and copied, commissioning Robert Ross to entrust it to a typewriting agency (CL: 514). As Guy and Small put it, 'Wilde's comments [in his letters] suggest that the manuscript was intended as a letter (and as such finished) and simultaneously as the draft for some possible future work' (Guy and Small 2000: 214). Wilde went to quite a lot of trouble to ensure that it survived (he knew enough about Douglas's temper not to trust the only copy to him), and part of the reason for this may well be that it was a rehearsal piece, a text that was serving multiple functions. It is the nearest thing Wilde wrote to an autobiography, but it was written under very difficult conditions, during the period of his imprisonment, and those conditions have a material effect on what he actually produced. It is an example of a text written under physical and emotional stress, part of the aim of which is to reaffirm the subject's subjectivity, and to resist the structures of subjection that are implicit in any prison regime. He also wrote into the text an *apologia pro vita sua*, an explanation of a sort, for his actions.

De Profundis has had a mixed reputation, and many critics have attacked it as an artistic failure, as an incoherent, unpalatable and false account of Wilde's life. Graham Hough, for example, in *The Last Romantics*, dismisses it as emetic posturing. He was writing in 1948 before the publication of the complete text of the letter (by Rupert Hart-Davis in 1962), but his comment is venomous in its distaste for what Wilde was and what he had done. Even more sympathetic critics, such as Jonathan Dollimore, have seen it as a 'conscious renunciation' of everything that Wilde had stood for before he was sent to prison (Dollimore 1991: 95). Commentators often suggest that the text has a divided aim – to blame Bosie for what had happened, and to reconstruct a positive image of Wilde's self – and in as much as it is divided, they regard it as bad art, a failure in Wilde's writing career. This assessment points us to one of the essential problems in literary autobiography, since autobiography is necessarily a form (or possibly a genre) pulled in two conflicting directions. On the one hand, the reader has expectations of a sincere expression of the self, while on the other she/he expects that the self will also be constructed in a self-consciously literary way. Autobiographical writing is always double, torn between style and sincerity – which are, of course, two of Wilde's key oppositions expressed throughout his writing.

The hostile responses to *De Profundis* come from two sources. In Hough's case, there is a distaste for the 'fact' of Wilde's sexuality. Homosexuality is seen as an inappropriate subject for any literary discussion. It is an illiberal view, cruel, unkind and unnecessary, though typical of the period in which he was writing. But other hostile responses have to do with a failure to understand the conditions in which Wilde was writing. When Wilde was sent to prison in May, 1895, it was under the rules of what was called penal servitude (as opposed to simple 'imprisonment'). Under the rules of imprisonment, a prisoner could be sentenced to any term between 3 and 5 years. He would be kept in solitary confinement for the first 9 months of his incarceration; but after that period he would be allowed to associate with other prisoners, work with them, talk to them, and receive a certain amount of education. Under the rules of penal servitude, on the other hand, a prisoner would be sentenced to a maximum of 2 years with hard labour. But the whole of that period would be spent in isolation, with severe penalties if, during the 1 hour of exercise allowed per day, he spoke to any other prisoner. As Regenia Gagnier shows, the prisoner's existence was one of monotony and silence, with a rigid regime of daily life, spent largely in a tiny cell, '13' × 7' × 9', with one window of opaque glass 6'9" above the floor':

> 6 am, clean cell; 7, porridge and brown bread; exercise for an hour, oakum picking till noon; dinner of bacon, beans bread (cold meat once a week); 12:30–6 pm, oakum picking; tea or gruel and eight

ounces of bread; 7 pm, lights out. No personal possessions were
allowed in the cell, which included only a plank bed, a blanket, a hard
pillow, and a small table. Each morning on pain of punishment, the
prisoner would arrange these items symmetrically for inspection . . .
One letter could be sent and received per quarter for the 'purpose of
enabling [prisoners] to keep up a connection with their respectable
friends and not that they might be kept informed of public events.'
No books were allowed the first month, during the second and third
only a Bible, a prayer-book, and a hymn-book. Afterwards, one book
a week from the prison-library was permitted.

(Gagnier 1986: 185)

The regime of penal servitude was so extreme that many prisoners
preferred to serve longer sentences under the rules of imprisonment;
and, indeed, the monotony, silence and solitude were known to be
prime causes of insanity among the prison population. The food
was also extremely bad and Wilde suffered – as almost all prisoners
did – from diarrhoea for the first few months of his imprisonment.
The unpleasantness of the condition was exacerbated by the fact that
prisoners were locked into their cells for most of the day, having only
a chamber pot to relieve themselves in. Wilde wrote movingly of the
stench in two letters he wrote to the *Daily Chronicle* about prison
reform when he was released. Prisoners who had hard labour attached
to their sentences had to pick oakum (separate strands of rotten rope)
or turn the crank or operate a treadmill. These were all useless forms
of labour with no useful end product: work was merely a punishment.
On the first day of his sentence, Wilde was also forced to bathe in
water that had already been used by other prisoners, had his hair cut
and was put into a prison uniform. Alongside the sheer tedium of an
unhygienic regime, there were also assaults on the bodily dignity of
the prisoner, rituals of humiliation and alienation from the image of
the former self. For a man like Wilde, whose image had been a very
large part of his public (and private) persona, this was a profound
humiliation. While one would wish to avoid snobbery, working-
class prisoners themselves could see that this regime was worse for a
middle-class man than it was for them; Wilde records how touched he
was by such an acknowledgement from a fellow prisoner, who risked
punishment to speak his sympathy for Wilde's plight.

These physical constraints were not the only constraints on Wilde as he composed the letter. The act of writing was supposedly forbidden to prisoners under Home Office regulations, except for the quarterly letter to one's respectable friends on the outside. But when Wilde was eventually moved to Reading, having served part of his sentence at Pentonville, the liberal governor, Major Nelson, made special provision for Wilde to be allowed to write, and to have more books than the official allowance. His reasoning was that this would enable to Wilde to continue his career as a writer on his release. But Wilde was still a prisoner, and therefore could not be allowed to do just what he pleased; and in a letter to the Prison Commissioners, Major Nelson explained: 'Each sheet [of paper] was carefully numbered before being issued and withdrawn each evening at locking and placed before me in the morning with the usual papers' (CL: 683n). Wilde, that is, was given one quarto sheet of paper per day. He had to hand the paper in at the end of each day, and he was not supposed to be given access to sheets that he had already written. It seems likely that Major Nelson did allow Wilde to see and correct his previous pages – the manuscript, as Holland and Hart-Davis suggest, contains evidence of annotation and changes, and some sheets are fair copies of earlier drafts. Nonetheless, Wilde was clearly working under very severe restraints, and under these conditions, it should come as no surprise that the piece is not a seamless whole.

When Wilde was released from prison in May 1897, he sent the manuscript to his friend Robert Ross with a covering letter explaining what the text was, and what Ross was to do with it. Wilde's instructions were that copies were to be taken from the manuscript, and then the original was to be sent to Lord Alfred Douglas. Wilde wrote to Ross on 1 April 1897 with his request:

> As regards the mode of copying: of course it is too long for any amanuensis to attempt. . . . I think the only thing to do is to be thoroughly modern, and to have it type-written. Of course, the manuscript should not pass out of your control, but could you not get Mrs Marshall to send down one of her type-writing girls – women are the most reliable, as they have no memory for the important – . . . to do it under your supervision. I assure you that the type-writing machine, when played with expression, is not more annoying than the piano when played by a sister or near relation. Indeed many, amongst those most devoted to domesticity, prefer it. . . . If the copying is

done at Hornton Street the lady type-writer may be fed through a
lattice like the Cardinals when they elect a Pope, till she comes out on
the balcony and can say to the world '*Habet Mundus Epistolam;*' for
indeed it is an Encyclical Letter, and as the Bulls of the Holy Father are
named from their opening words, it may be spoken of as the *Epistola:
In Carcere et Vinculis* [Letter: in Prison and in Chains].

(CL: 781)

In the same letter, Wilde explains his motivation for having written
the letter. He tells Ross that it is the only document that 'really
gives any explanation of my extraordinary behaviour' with regard to
Queensberry and Alfred Douglas.

When you have read the letter, you will see the psychological
explanation of a course of conduct that from the outside seems
a combination of absolute idiocy with vulgar bravado. Some day
the truth will have to be known . . . I am not prepared to sit in the
grotesque pillory they put me into for all time: for the simple reason
that I inherited from my father and my mother a name of high
distinction in literature and art, and I cannot, for eternity, allow that
name to be the shield and catspaw of the Queensberrys. I don't defend
my conduct. I explain it.

(CL: 780)

In these two extracts, we can see Wilde first of all reassuming his guise
as a wit; and secondly giving a genre (a letter) and a title (*Epistola: In
Carcere et Vinculis*) to his text.

In fact, the title *De Profundis* was Robert Ross's invention. In the
event, Ross kept the manuscript version and posted a typescript to
Douglas (which Douglas claimed he never received). In 1905 Ross
edited the manuscript for publication (Guy and Small speculate that
he may have been using a copy that Wilde himself had corrected
and edited), deleting almost all the references that could specifically
identify anyone in the Queensberry family which he published as
De Profundis. Then, in 1912, he presented the manuscript to the
British Library with instructions that it should be sealed for 50 years
– that is, until all the people that Wilde named in the letter would be
dead. *De Profundis* is the opening of the Vulgate (or Roman Catholic)
Bible's version of Psalm 130: 'Out of the depths I cry to thee, O Lord;

Lord hear my prayer'. (The Vulgate is a Latin and therefore Roman Catholic translation of the Bible.) In giving this title to Wilde's letter, Ross was doing a number of things. He was explicitly associating Wilde with Roman Catholicism and the traditions of confession – justifiably, perhaps, because Wilde did become a Catholic on his deathbed and was in a papal frame of mind when he sent Ross the manuscript. But he was also asserting its genre more strongly: an auto-biography that is also a confession. The confession is supposed to be a narrative that combines both sincerity and coherence. Wilde, as the extracts from his letter to Ross quoted above shows, also associated his letter with Catholicism. But his version is much more grandiose and satirical. He jokingly makes himself a secular pontiff making doctrinal rulings in the form of an Encyclical Letter to the Church of his few remaining disciples. Perhaps more importantly, Wilde's title for his prison letter says two very specific things: that it is a letter; and that it is a letter produced in the extreme conditions of prison and chains. A letter is not necessarily a confession – nor is it necessarily an explanation. One of the effects of Ross's title was that it sends confused signals out to the public about the text's genre. These messages may at least partially account for some of the critical hostility – Ross's title signals one thing, but the letter itself is quite another.

It was not until 1962 that the full text of the letter became available to the public. And by then, because the public and scholars were used to the idea that it was all about Wilde posing as the figure of Christ, critical positions had become entrenched. The fact that it still appears under Ross's title, rather than Wilde's, probably continues to compound the problem of interpretation.

The Construction of a Relative Self: De Profundis

Modern life is complex and relative; those are its two distinguishing notes; to render the first we require atmosphere with its subtlety of *nuances*, of suggestion, of strange perspectives; as for the second, we require background. That is why sculpture has ceased to be a representative art and why music is a representative art and why literature is, and has been, and always will remain the supreme representative art.

(CW: 1012)

Whatever happens to another happens to oneself.

(CL: 1027)

De Profundis consists of two strands, one that enumerates multiple instances of Bosie's bad behaviour, and one in which Wilde seeks to move on from the past by reference to an ideal future with Christ at its heart. The two strands, which sometimes shade into each other, appear to be absolutely at odds in logical terms with any notion of coherence, and with any sense that what Wilde is producing for us is the spectacle of an explanation. However, what is particularly interesting about Wilde's position is the extent to which his notion of the self is dependent on the notion of the other. Wilde is presenting us with a discursive self, a self created through language, in a kind of conversation (a dramatic monologue, perhaps, since Wilde writes into the text his predictions of Bosie's response to it). Because it is a self dependent on language, communication and interpretation, it is a contingent rather than an essential self.

That the self is not 'essence' is something that Wilde had constantly reiterated throughout his writings, in particular his sense of the distinction between the mask and the person that stands behind it. The particularity of the prison situation makes this even more an acute revelation. Who is Oscar Wilde when his name has been taken away from him? (He is called C.3.3. after the number on his cell door.) Who is Oscar Wilde when his name has been removed from his plays in the West End? When his children have been removed from his jurisdiction by court order? When his mother has died, and he has been unable to go to her funeral because he is in prison? When all his goods have been sold in order to pay for his bankruptcy? When his image and clothing have been taken away from him? In other words, what does a self whose markers of identity have been removed consist of? In all the terms of the world, Wilde has become nothing in his prison guise except a prisoner, defined entirely by his crime and his punishment, defined, not by himself, but by others. As a man, a father, a husband, a son, an economic entity, a writer, an image, he has been collapsed into the image of the prisoner with no name except his number, C.3.3.

In these special circumstances, for Wilde the self must then reside elsewhere, and he posits a self that exists in memory, and a self that will exist perhaps in the future through an act of imaginative resistance to the position of the prisoner, as he identifies himself with

Christ. Of the two selves, critics have disliked the vitriol addressed at Douglas, who represents in the text Wilde's past self; and they have disliked also the hubris of a self-identification with Christ. But they have seldom seen that the two selves arise directly out of the conditions in which Wilde found himself.

Most of the first part of *De Profundis* consists of a minutely detailed rendition of Wilde's life with Douglas. It includes a wealth of financial detail; lists of what they did and where, very carefully recorded with dates recalled as exactly as possible; specific incidents in which Bosie misbehaved; and a precise record of the consequences of Wilde's relationship – including his bankruptcy, his projected divorce, the loss of his children and his current position in the 'house of detention.' Regenia Gagnier describes this minutiae as posing 'a total imaginative world against the frozen time and alien space of imprisonment. . . . Wilde forces the presence of Douglas in the prose in order to make the pre-prison Wilde a reality' (Gagnier 1986: 187). What becomes clear then from this wealth of detail is that for Wilde to 'know himself', as he puts it, he must also recall Bosie's self: there is a very profound identification between the two men in the text, which dramatizes the position that to know oneself, one must also know the other – indeed, that the self may be entirely dependent on the other for its definition. Hence the proposition that the self is at once what the other is not, and the other is whatever is 'not-self'. In the oscillation between these two binary poles, Wilde presents a version of self that deconstructs itself. Definition – including self-definition – becomes relative and open ended. The self must act and define itself by appropriating the other to a greater or lesser degree, and self affirmation depends on that appropriation of the other. In telling Douglas's story, Wilde is appropriating events for himself and is thereby also telling his own story through the story of the other.

The confusion between self and other becomes particularly apparent in the grammatical contortions of Wilde's narrative in which the subject and the object of the sentence (roughly equivalent to Wilde and Bosie) collapse into each other.

> I will begin by telling you that I blame myself terribly. As I sit here in this dark cell in convict clothes, a disgraced and ruined man, I blame myself. In the perturbed and fitful nights of anguish, in the long monotonous days of pain, it is myself I blame. I blame myself for

allowing an unintellectual friendship, a friendship whose primary aim was not the creation and contemplation of beautiful things, entirely to dominate my life. . . . I blame myself for having allowed you to bring me to utter and discreditable financial ruin. . . . But most of all I blame myself for the entire ethical degradation I allowed you to bring on me. The basis of character is will power, and my will power became absolutely subject to yours.

(CW: 981–4)

Grammatically, Wilde signals that subject and object are the same; that self and other are inseparable, that there is a sense in which Wilde became Bosie.

To be Bosie, however, is clearly not a desirable thing to be. Bosie is selfish, extravagant, rude, unsympathetic, non-intellectual and wasteful. To attach one's own self to Bosie's 'other' is to risk becoming all of those things. And so Wilde poses an alternative imaginative version of the world and the self in the figure of Christ. Christ has many advantages here: 'There is something so unique about Christ' says Wilde in a litotes that is not only typically satirical, but which also borders on the profane. One element of Christ's uniqueness is that he represents a figure of forgiveness (hence Ross's use of a psalm about forgiveness as his title for the work), and if Wilde is to cease to be Bosie, he has to detach himself from Bosie's self by means that Bosie himself would not use – Bosie is an unforgiving figure and Christ is the supreme figure of forgiveness in Western culture. Inside his autobiography, Wilde writes other biographies of both Bosie and Christ. Where Bosie represents all that is ugly and painful, and is a bar to Wilde's art, Wilde's Christ is an aesthetic figure, a supreme artist in his own right. Norbert Kohl has suggested that for Wilde Christ is the paradigm figure of the suffering artist (Kohl 1989), and he identifies him as a poet. Indeed, as Richard Ellmann notes, the one aspect of Christ that is given no significance in Wilde's account is his divinity – precisely the aspect of Christ that ought to be most important in conventional readings of his meaning (Ellmann 1988). For Wilde, Christ's story ends with 'the stone rolled over the door of the sepulchre', not with divine manifestation of the Resurrection, in which his meaning resides for most people.

It is personality that matters most here. Wilde's narrative insists that Christ's most important value is that he exemplified imaginative sympathy with suffering – precisely what Bosie is incapable of. (Wilde continually castigates Bosie for his failure to imagine what Wilde is feeling now.) Christ's sympathy made his life into a work of art, into 'the most wonderful of poems.' His miracles have nothing to do with divinity. They are dependent on personality.

> His miracles seem to me to be as exquisite as spring and quite as natural. I see no difficulty in believing that such was the charm of his personality that his mere presence could bring peace to souls in anguish, and that those who touched his garments or his hands forgot their pain; . . . or that when he taught on the hillside the multitude forgot their hunger and thirst and the cares of the world, and that to his friends who listened to him as he sat at meat the coarse food seemed delicate, and the water had the taste of good wine, and the whole house became full of the odour and sweetness of nard.
>
> (CW: 1029)

What Wilde is describing as Christ's personality, is of course, very close to the common perception of his own. His conversation, the stories he told others, all acted like a charm on those who heard him. Even the Marquess of Queensberry, when he met Wilde for the first time, was charmed, writing to Bosie: 'I don't wonder that you are so fond of him. He is a wonderful man' (Ellmann 1988: 393). In this text then, man is not made in the image of God; Christ is remade in the image of Wilde. 'Christ is the most supreme of individualists', he wrote (CW: 1029).

Paradoxically, it is partially the invocation of Christ that enables Wilde to avoid the confessional mode. He does not confess past faults, except in as much as he 'blames himself' for his friendship with Bosie, thereby rendering Bosie the cause of his crimes. The conventional narratives of confession and of crime and punishment are invoked, but not produced. For example, Wilde produces a list of things that are supposed to help the fallen sinner, but which do not help him. 'Neither religion, morality nor reason can help me at all' (CW: 1019). But he also says, 'I don't regret for a single moment having lived for pleasure. I did it to the full, as one should do everything that one does. . . . But to have continued the same life would have been wrong, because it would have been limiting' (CW: 1026), which makes clear that repentance, a new mode of life is merely another experience rather than a distinctively moral choice. And he speaks of himself as a 'born antinomian . . . made for exceptions, not for laws' (CW: 1019). There is, throughout *De Profundis*, a resistance to conventional narratives of the self, which is why I would argue that far from being an unconsidered trifle and in opposition to the rest of Wilde's oeuvre, it is a central restatement of the positions he adopted throughout his life.

Character and Personality

In the Preface to *Dorian Gray*, Wilde wrote that the aim of art is to 'reveal art and conceal the artist.' And yet, his writings also positively invite a biographical approach, since Wilde also argues that art is the expression of the artist's perfected personality. It is in his choice of the word 'personality' that I think we must seek to understand Wilde's position, in relation to both art and to the defining of the self. For despite the textuality of his own life, Wilde was not a character in a three-volume novel; and he very rarely uses the word character at all. Is there any essential difference between character and personality?

The English word 'character' has its origins in the Greek word *kharakter*, meaning something impressed or stamped. In the *Oxford English Dictionary*, the first definition refers one to printing; the second defines character as a biological term, meaning the collective peculiarities of a species or race. The third usage originates from the idea of the written testimonial to a person's essential qualities; servants in eighteenth-century England were given 'characters' by their employers, which attested to their moral qualities – similar to the modern-day reference. Only with the fourth definition do we move distinctly to the world of literature, and our usage of the word in literary criticism. The etymological investigation suggests that the word character implies stability and knowability. Character is stamped or impressed through the individual like the lettering in a stick of rock. Therefore, it is a word better suited to fiction than to real people whose knowability and stability must, after all, always be open to question.

Personality on the other hand comes from a Latin root, *persona*, meaning in the first instance 'actor's mask', and then increasingly the sense becomes the public face, the face that one presents to the world, which may not quite be the same thing as one's reality. The difference between the two terms is that personality refers not to the essential being, the inner core of self, but to a role that can be adopted and put aside at will. Consequently, a self figured as personality is potentially inconsistent, and knowable only in a conditional way, for the moments during which that particular mask is being worn. Wilde comments in *De Profundis*: 'Behind Joy and Laughter there may be a temperament, coarse, hard and callous. But behind Sorrow there is always Sorrow. Pain, unlike Pleasure, wears no mask' (CW: 1024). And there is a sense in which that statement stakes a claim for the authenticity of emotion and sincerity of expression of *De Profundis*. But in speaking of the mask, Wilde also implies that even though the naked face is sincere, it may yet reassume its disguise. While on the one hand he asks his addressee to see him unadorned – naked, as it were – and is thus risking his self (Douglas commented to Wilde that when he was not on his pedestal he was not interesting, Wilde recalls with bitterness), he also dramatises in *De Profundis* his unwillingness to occupy this position for long. He reassembles a personality that he then associates implicitly and explicitly with the personality of Christ, replacing himself in the process on the artistic pedestal from which scandal had removed him. He is asserting that the maskless face of sorrow is not a permanent condition. It does not reveal character – essence – but is an alternative persona, which is soon rejected.

If the letter is inconsistent in that it is not merely a humble confession, nor just the letter of an injured lover, nor a therapy, nor an autobiographical explanation, it is at least consistent with Wilde's view that each of these alternatives is just one possibility among many. A self may write (or be written into) all of these genres in turn. Life is not something that can be seen steadily and whole, as it 'really is'. Instead, it has to be read sequentially as a series of possibilities. The biographer or critic who seeks a single or simple explanation for any life is treacherous, like the Judas who writes the biography – 'a truth in art is that whose contradictory is also true'. Wilde's view is that lives, even narrated lives, must resist the closure of *the* authoritative interpretation. The self is always multiple, and therefore knowledge of it is always deferred. And the self is always a performance at least as much as it is an expression of any stabilized identity.

The Ballad of Reading Gaol *(1897)*

De Profundis was produced within the prison system, a response to the conditions of imprisonment, but also an attempt to imagine alternative realities. On his release from prison, however, Wilde returned to the subject, in his last major work – *The Ballad of Reading Gaol*. The *Ballad* has a stronger claim perhaps to being the conscious renunciation of Wilde's aesthetic theory. In a letter to Laurence Housman (A. E. Housman's brother) in August 1897, shortly after his release, Wilde wrote in praise of the 'lovely, lyrical poems' of *A Shropshire Lad*, and went on to describe his own new project:

> with regard to what you ask me about myself – well, I am occupied in finishing a poem, terribly realistic for me, and drawn from actual experience, a sort of denial of my own philosophy of art in many ways. I hope it is good, but every night I hear cocks crowing in Berneval, so I am afraid I have denied myself, and would weep bitterly, if I had not wept away all my tears. I will send it to you, if you will allow me, when it appears.
>
> (CL: 928)

The poem to which he refers in this letter was *The Ballad of Reading Gaol*, his last literary production, eventually published in February 1898, without Wilde's name on the title page, but under the imprint of his prison number, C.3.3. Wilde feared it was a betrayal of his aesthetic principles, commenting to Ross in a letter (1 October 1897) that although parts of the Ballad were very good, he would 'never again out-Kipling Henley' (CL: 950), a remark that speaks to the fear that the poem was 'terribly realistic' in the manner of the contemporary poets Rudyard Kipling or W.E. Henley, rather than 'fantastic' as *The Sphinx* of 1894 had been.

Wilde hoped that his ballad would go some way towards rehabilitating his reputation both as an artist and as a man. He wanted to show that the years in prison had not destroyed him – and in that aim, the poem was not successful. Although the reviews were generally quite favourable, Wilde was never to return to England or to his pre-prison productivity; and even the poem's relative financial success was not nearly enough to discharge the bankruptcy attendant on his prosecution of the Marquess of Queensberry. Moreover, his reputation was not rescued by the poem, since his name did not appear on the title page of his poem until the seventh printing of June 1899, when the poem's success was assured.

Reviewers noted the range of influences on the poem, suggesting links with Thomas Hood's poem 'The Dream of Eugene Aram, the Murderer', Rudyard Kipling's *Barrack Room Ballads* (and in particular the poem called 'Danny Deever', which is also about a murderer), and Coleridge's *Rime of the Ancient Mariner*. The reviews speak of being impressed by the achievement of the poem, but also of disliking the tone in which it was written. For example, the reviewer 'S. G.' in the *Pall Mall Gazette* said:

> The most remarkable poem that has appeared this year is, of course, *The Ballad of Reading Gaol*. It has been much written about, but no-one has commented . . . on the curious parallel between it and Mr. Kipling's 'Danny Deever', the grim lyric which stands first in *Barrack Room Ballads*. The difference is just this: 'Danny Deever' – ugly if you like, but a real poem – is a conspicuously manly piece of work; *The Ballad of Reading Gaol*, with all its feverish energy, is unmanly. The central emotion is the physical horror of death, when death comes, not as a relief or in a whirl of excitement, but as an abrupt shock to be dreaded. That the emotion is genuine admits of no doubt; but it is one very fit to be concealed.
>
> (CH: 221–2)

It is a moot point to what extent the reviewers knew that C.3.3. was Wilde, though it must have been a kind of open secret. If readers knew the identity of the poet, they would have found it virtually impossible not to comment in the knowledge of his 'crime' and earlier reputation. The ghosts of earlier criticism (the 'unmanly manhood' comments that greeted *Poems*) haunt this particular commentary. It seems to modern readers an extremely odd thing to say, too – as if the 'horror of death' is an unnatural emotion that should be concealed. The construction of masculinity in the period remains an issue that inflects how Wilde is read. 'Danny Deever' is a much more brutal poem because it is brief, restrained, and its speakers are inarticulate, so their horror is not expressed in their own language, but left to the reader to intuit. The 'stiff-upper lip' of Kipling's poem speaks to conventional masculinity in ways that the extended 'sensitivity' of Wilde's poem does not.

   The Ballad is a poem about guilt – not just the specific guilt of a particular criminal who is to hang in Reading Gaol, but a universal guilt in which all men are implicated, though not all men suffer for their guilt.

> Yet each man kills the thing he loves,
> By each let this be heard,
> Some do it with a bitter look,
> Some with a flattering word,
> The coward does it with a kiss,
> The brave man with a sword!
>
>   (CW: 884)

The guilt of the particular case is symptomatic of general guilt. And, as S. G. suggested, Wilde does indeed dwell on the physical horror of death by hanging, writing of the 'swollen purple throat/And stark and staring eyes' three times over in the poem. What the soldier 'did not do' ('he did not wear his scarlet coat') is linked to what 'does not' happen to the rest of mankind despite the universality of guilt: though each man kills the thing he loves, 'Yet each man does not die':

> He does not die a death of shame
> On a day of dark disgrace,
> Nor have a noose about his neck,
> Nor a cloth upon his face,
> Nor drop feet foremost through the floor
> Into an empty space.
>
>   (CW: 884)

The repeated negatives emphasize the contrast between the expectations of innocent and guilty men. Where the prisoner's horizons have been limited to 'the little tent of blue/That prisoners call the sky', those of the free man are unbounded. Where the condemned man waits only for the macabre simplicity of death as expressed in the above-quoted stanza (dramatized in the quietly violent monosyllabic language), the free man has unlimited possibilities. By dwelling on the possibilities of one life and death, Wilde points the contrasts between this and the pleasures available to men he characterizes as equally guilty.

Wilde wants in this poem to explore the paradoxical relationship between innocence and guilt, mutually dependent oppositions, and he does so by disrupting the simple narrative of cause and effect on which the law depends – crime produces guilt produces punishment, but each man is equally guilty. The logic of cause and effect is problematic, signalled in the illogical connection the poem makes between blood and wine (both are red) which is the reason that the former soldier 'did not wear his scarlet coat'. He asks his readers to share his own uncertainty about innocence and guilt and thereby seeks to implicate them in crime ('for each man kills the thing he loves') and its punishment:

> And I and all the other souls in pain
> Who tramped the other ring
> Forgot if we ourselves had done
> A great or little thing,
> And watched with dull amaze
> The man who had to swing.
>
> And strange it was to see him pass
> With a step so light and gay,
> And strange it was to see him look
> So wistfully at the day,
> And strange it was to think that he
> Had such a debt to pay.

(CW: 886)

Throughout his career, Wilde resisted totalizing narratives that authoritatively explained everything. Rather, his aim was to show that selfhood and its narratives should be multiple. Prisoner C.3.3., found guilty and explained away to prison, in his prison writings asked his readers to see that there is more to it than straight-line narratives of cause and effect. There is romance as realism; and innocence can only be defined in relation to guilt or experience. He asks us to recognize that we are also implicated; and as such, he threatened the common-sense version of the world, of masculinity, of art, seeing such things as prescriptive and over-determined. 'The final mystery is oneself', he wrote in *De Profundis*. And the claim that anything can be fully known is what he resisted most forcefully.

Notes

Note to Introduction

1. There are a number of other useful books that offer some insight into the context of late-nineteenth-century Britain in which Wilde lived, loved and worked. For those seeking information about the general cultural milieu, Karl Beckson's (1993) *London in the 1890s: A Cultural History* and John Stokes' (1989) *In the Nineties* – both are extraordinarily helpful resources. The homosexual context, along with the histories of several other contemporary same-sex scandals can be read in Morris Kaplan's (2005) *Sodom on the Thames* – a useful source for the general reader; and in Matt Cook's (2003) *London and the Culture of Homosexuality* for a more academically nuanced account. Wilde's sojourn in America is treated in exquisite detail in Gary Schmidgall's (1995) *The Stranger Wilde*.

Note to Chapter Two – Prose: Critical

1. The complete Oxford University Press edition of Wilde's complete works has not yet published Wilde's collected journalism. There are a few collections of his journalism, but they are clearly not complete at all. The best of them is John W. Jackson's (1991) *Aristotle at Afternoon Tea.*

Notes to Chapter Three – Prose: Short Fictional

1. Made popular in the late nineteenth century by Wagner, *Venus and Tannhauser* tells the story of how the Christian knight Tannhauser seeks the love of Venus; the pope tells him that his action is unforgivable, heretical and profane, and will only be forgiven when the pope's staff flowers; which it does rather to his annoyance.

2. There is not space here to go into all the details behind this brief 'history'. Interested readers can find out more by referring to John Sutherland (2005) *Victorian Fiction: Writers, Publishers, Readers*; Richard D. Altick (1957) *The English Common Reader*; Altick's (2000) essay 'Publishing'; and John Feather (2005) *A History of British Publishing*. For more information about the context of the Victorian short story, see Emma Liggins, Andrew Maunder and Ruth Robbins (2011) *The British Short Story*.

Bibliography

Adams, James E. (1995), *Dandies and Desert Saints: Styles of Victorian Manhood*, Ithaca and London: Cornell University Press.

Altick, Richard D. (1957), *The English Common Reader: A Social History of the Mass Reading Public, 1800–1900*, Chicago: University of Chicago Press.

Altick, Richard D. (2000), 'Publishing', in Herbert F. Tucker (ed.), *A Companion to Victorian Literature and Culture*, London: Blackwell: pp. 289–306.

Arnold, Matthew (1972), *Selected Criticism of Matthew Arnold*, Christopher Ricks (ed.), New York: Signet Books.

Ash, Russell (n.d.), *Sir Lawrence Alma-Tadema,* London: Michael Joseph.

Attridge, Derek (ed.) (1992), *Jacques Derrida: Acts of Literature*, London: Routledge.

Bartlett, Neil (1988), *Who was that man? A Present for Mr Oscar Wilde*, London: Serpent's Tail.

Beckson, Karl (ed.) (1970), *Oscar Wilde: The Critical Heritage*, London: Routledge and Kegan Paul.

Beckson, Karl (1993), *London in the 1890s: A Cultural History*, New York: W. W. Norton and Co.

Botting, Fred (1995), *Gothic*, London: Routledge.

Brake, Laurel (1994), *Subjugated Knowledges: Journalism, Literature and Gender in the Nineteenth Century*, Basingstoke: Macmillan.

Brantlinger, Patrick (1996), 'Imperial Gothic: Atavism and the Occult in the British Adventure Novel, 1880–1914' in Lyn Pykett (ed.), *Reading Fin de Siècle Fictions*, London: Longman: pp. 184–209.

Bristow, Joseph (1997), *Sexuality*, London: Routledge (New Critical Idiom Series).

Cohen, Ed (1993), *Talk on the Wilde Side: Towards a Genealogy of a Discourse on Male Sexualities*, London: Routledge.

Cohen, Philip K. (1978), *The Moral Vision of Oscar Wilde*, London: London and Associated University Presses.

Cook, Matt (2003), *London and the Culture of Homosexuality*, Cambridge: Cambridge University Press.

Danson, Lawrence (1997), *Wilde's Intentions: The Artist in his Criticism*, Oxford: Clarendon Press.

Dellamorra, Richard (1990), *Masculine Desire: The Sexual Politics of Victorian Aestheticism*, London and Chapel Hill: University of California Press.

Derrida, Jacques (1980), 'The Law of Genre', Avital Ronell (trans.), *Critical Inquiry*, 7, i: 55–81.

Dijkstra, Bram (1986), *Idols of Perversity: Fantasies of Feminine Evil in Fin-de-Siècle Culture*, Oxford and New York: Oxford University Press.

Dollimore, Jonathan (1991), *Sexual Dissidence: Augustine to Wilde, Freud to Foucault*, Oxford: Clarendon Press.

Ellmann, Richard (1988), *Oscar Wilde*. Harmondsworth: Penguin.

Eltis, Sos (1996), *Revising Wilde: Society and Subversion in the Plays of Oscar Wilde*, Oxford: Clarendon Press.

Feather, John (2005), *A History of British Publishing*, London: Routledge.

Flanagan-Behrendt, Patricia (1991), *Oscar Wilde: Eros and Aesthetics*, London: Macmillan.

Foucault, Michel (1979; 1984), *The History of Sexuality: An Introduction*, Robert Hurley (trans.), Harmondsworth: Penguin.

Freud, Sigmund (1990), 'The Uncanny' [1919] in *Art and Literature*, The Penguin Freud Library, Vol. 14, Harmondsworth: Penguin: pp. 339–76.

Gagnier, Regenia (1986), *Idylls of the Marketplace: Oscar Wilde and the Victorian Public*, Aldershot: Scolar Press.

Greer, Germaine (2003), *The Boy*, London: Thames and Hudson.

Guy, Josephine M. and Ian Small (2000), *Oscar Wilde's Profession: Writing and the Culture Industry in the Late Nineteenth Century*, Oxford: Oxford University Press.

Guy, Josephine M. (1998), 'Self Plagiarism, Creativity and Craftsmanship in Oscar Wilde', *English Literature in Transition*, 41, i: 6–23.

Hoare, Philip (1997), *Wilde's Last Stand: Decadence, Conspiracy and the First World War*, London: Duckworth.

Holland, Merlin (ed.) (1994), *The Complete Works of Oscar Wilde*, Glasgow: HarperCollins.

Holland, Merlin and Rupert Hart-Davis (eds) (2000), *The Complete Letters of Oscar Wilde*, London: Fourth Estate.

Hough, Graham (1949; 1979), *The Last Romantics*, London: Duckworth.

Hyde, H. Montgomery (1948), *The Trials of Oscar Wilde*, London: William Hodge and Co.

Hyde, H. Montgomery (1962), *Famous Trials: Oscar Wilde*, Harmondsworth: Penguin.

Jackson, Rosemary (1981), *Fantasy: The Literature of Subversion*, London: Routledge.

Kaplan, Morris B. (2005), *Sodom on the Thames: Sex, Love and Scandal in Wilde Times*, Ithaca and London: Cornell University Press.

Kaye, Richard A. (2004), 'Gay Studies/Queer Theory and Oscar Wilde' in Frederick S. Roden (ed.), *Oscar Wilde Studies*, Basingstoke: Palgrave: pp. 189–223).

Kermode, Frank (1957; 1986), *Romantic Image*, London: RKP Ark Paperbacks.

Killeen, Jarlath (2002), *The Faiths of Oscar Wilde: Catholicism, Folklore and Ireland*, Basingstoke: Palgrave Macmillan.

Knox, Melissa (1994), *Oscar Wilde: A Long and Lovely Suicide*, New Haven and London: Yale University Press.

Kohl, Norbert (1989), *Oscar Wilde, The Works of a Conformist Rebel.* Cambridge: Cambridge University Press.

Ledger, Sally and Roger Luckhust (eds) (2000), *The Fin de Siècle: A Reader in Cultural History, 1880–1900*, Oxford: Oxford University Press.

Liggins, Emma, Andrew Maunder and Ruth Robbins (2011), *The British Short Story*. Basingstoke: Palgrave.

Marsh, Jan (1987), *Pre-Raphaelite Women: Images of Femininity in Pre-Raphaelite Art*, London: Guild Publishing.

McCormack, Jerusha (1997), 'Wilde's Fiction(s)' in Peter Raby (ed.), *The Cambridge Companion to Oscar Wilde*, Cambridge: Cambridge University Press: pp. 102–17).

McCormack, Jerusha (ed.) (1998), *Wilde the Irishman*, New Haven and London: Yale University Press.

Mikhail, E. H. (ed.) (1979), *Oscar Wilde: Interviews and Recollections*, 2 volumes, London: Macmillan.

Mort, Frank (1987; 2nd edn 2000), *Dangerous Sexualities: Medico-Moral Politics in England since 1850*, London: Routledge.

Naasaar, Christopher (1974), *Into the Demon Universe: a Literary Exploration of Oscar Wilde*, New Haven: Yale University Press.

Nead, Lynda (1988), *Myths of Sexuality: Representations of Women in Victorian Britain*, Oxford: Basil Blackwell.

Nead, Lynda (1992), *The Female Nude: Art, Obscenity and Sexuality*, London: Routledge.

Ong, Walter J. (1982), *Orality and Literacy: The Technologizing of the Word*, London: Methuen.

Pater, Walter (1980), *The Renaissance: Studies in Art and Poetry, the 1893 Text*, Donald L. Hill (ed.), Berkley and London: University of California Press.

Pine, Richard (1995), *The Thief of Reason: Oscar Wilde and Modern Ireland*, Dublin: Gill and Macmillan.

Poe, Edgar Allan (1967), *Selected Writings*, David Galloway (ed.), Harmondsworth: Penguin.

Powell, Kerry (1990), *Oscar Wilde and the Theatre of the 1890s*, Cambridge: Cambridge University Press.

Pykett, Lyn (ed.) (1996), *Reading Fin de Siècle Fictions*, London: Longman.

Raby, Peter (ed.) (1997), *The Cambridge Companion to Oscar Wilde*, Cambridge: Cambridge University Press.

Ransome, Arthur ([1912] 1913), *Oscar Wilde, A Critical Study*, London: Methuen and Co.

Robbins, Ruth (1997), 'Oscar Wilde: Before the Law', *New Formations*, 32, Autumn Winter: 99–108.

Robbins, Ruth (2000), 'The Genders of Socialism: Oscar Wilde and Eleanor Marx', in John Stokes (ed.), *Eleanor Marx: Life, Works, Contacts*, London: Ashgate: pp. 99–112.

Robbins, Ruth (2003), *Pater to Forster, 1873–1924*, Basingstoke: Palgrave

Roden, Frederick S. (ed.) (2004), *Oscar Wilde Studies*. Basingstoke: Palgrave.

Ruskin, John (1904), *Modern Painters*, Volume 3 (1856), in *The Works of John Ruskin: Library Edition*, E. T. Cook and Alexander Wedderburn (eds), Volume 5, London: George Allen.

Schmidgall, Gary (1995), *The Stranger Wilde: Interpreting Oscar*, New York: Plume.

Sedgwick, Eve Kosofsky (1980), *The Coherence of Gothic Conventions*, London and New York: Methuen.

Sedgwick, Eve Kosofsky (1985), *Between Men: English Literature and Male Homosocial Desire*, New York: University of Columbia Press.

Sedgwick, Eve Kosofksy (1994), *Epistemology of the Closet*, Harmondsworth: Penguin.

Shewan, Robert (1977), *Oscar Wilde: Art and Egotism*, London: Macmillan.

Showalter, Elaine (1991), *Sexual Anarchy: Gender and Culture at the Fin de Siècle*, London: Bloomsbury.

Sinfield, Alan (1994), *The Wilde Century: Effeminacy, Oscar Wilde and the Queer Moment*, London: Cassell.

Sloan, John (2003), *Authors in Context: Oscar Wilde*, Oxford: Oxford World's Classics.

Small, Ian (2000), *Oscar Wilde: Recent Research*, Greensboro: ELT Press.

Smith, Alison (1996), *The Victorian Nude: Sexuality, Morality and Art*, Manchester: Manchester University Press.

Stokes, John (1989), *In the Nineties*, Hemel Hempstead: Harvester Wheatsheaf.

Stokes, John (1996), *Oscar Wilde: Myths, Miracles and Imitations*, Cambridge: Cambridge University Press.

Sutherland, John (2005, 2nd edn), *Victorian Fiction: Writers, Publishers, Readers*. Basingstoke: Palgrave.

Thompson, E. P. (1977), *William Morris: Romantic to Revolutionary*, London: Merlin Press.

Thornton, R. K. R (1979), '"Decadence" in Later Nineteenth-Century England', in Ian Fletcher (ed.), *Decadence and the 1890s*, London: Edward Arnold.

Tydeman, William (ed.) (1982), *Wilde: Comedies*, Casebook Series. London: Macmillan.

Varty, Anne (1998), *A Preface to Oscar Wilde*, London: Longman.

Walkowitz, Judith R. (1992), *City of Dreadful Delight: Narratives of Sexual Danger in Late-Victorian London,* London: Virago.

Warner, Eric and Graham Hough (eds) (1983), *Strangeness and Beauty: An Anthology of Aesthetic Criticism, 1840–1910*, 2 volumes. Cambridge: Cambridge University Press.

Warwick, Alexandra (2007), *Oscar Wilde*, Tavistock: Northcote House, Writers and their Work Series.

Weeks, Jeffrey (1977), *Coming Out: Homosexual Politics in Britain from the Nineteenth Century to the Present*, London: Quartet.

Wilde, Oscar (1994), *The Complete Works of Oscar Wilde*, Merlin Holland (ed.), Edinburgh: HarperCollins.

Wilde, Oscar (1991), *Aristotle at Afternoon Tea: The Rare Oscar Wilde*, John Wyse Jackson (ed.), London: Fourth Estate.

Wilde, Oscar (2010), *The Sphinx*, with illustrations by Charles Ricketts, Fascsimile Edition, Nicholas Franckel (ed.), Houston, Texas: Rice University Press.

Williams, Raymond (1988), *Keywords: A Vocabulary of Culture and Society*, revised edn, London: Fontana.

Wood, Julia (2007), *The Resurrection of Oscar Wilde: A Cultural Afterlife*, Lutterworth, UK: Lutterworth Press.

Wordsworth, William and Samuel Taylor Coleridge (1991), *Lyrical Ballads*, R. L. Brett (ed.), London: Routledge.

Worth, Katharine (1983), *Modern Dramatists: Oscar Wilde*, London and Basingstoke: Macmillan.

Yeats, W. B. (1966), *Autobiographies*, London: Macmillan.

Index